Table of Contents

Acknowledgments 2
Dedication 3
Section 1: Pancakes, Waffles & French Toast 4
Section 2: Pastries 36
Section 3: Skillet Breakfast and Omelets 70
Section 4: Quiche and Benedicts 82
Section 5: Sandwiches and Wraps 96
Section 6: Side Dishes 110
Section 7: Drinks 121
 Index: 131

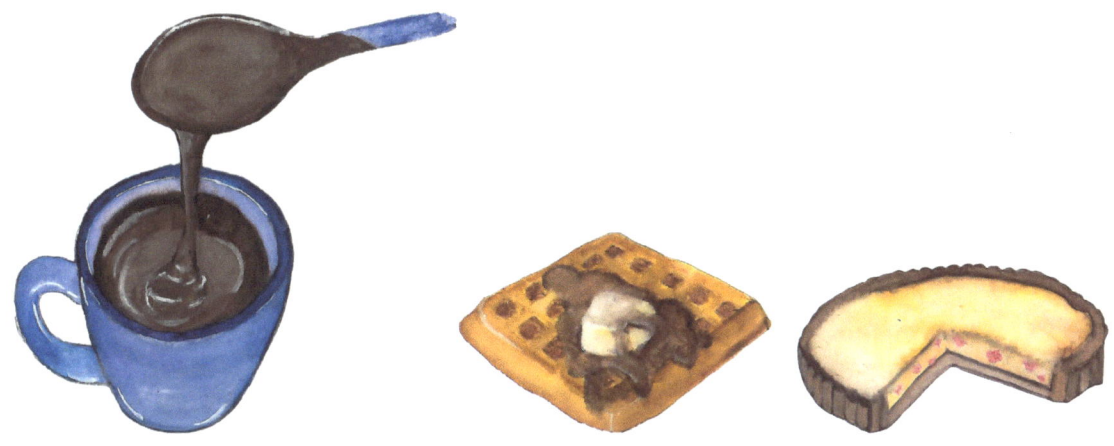

Acknowledgments

I would like to thank everyone who had a role in making this cookbook possible. My parents, Dave and Linda who supported me with love and understanding all my life and continue to encourage me to follow my dreams.

The love of my life, soul mate, and best friend, Saul Roberts who has loved me unconditionally and shown such a deep level of support as I worked tirelessly on this cookbook.

Finally, my dear friend of 20 years, Kevin Hagan who has supported my writing and given honest feedback during my writing process.

Thank you all for your unwavering support, I feel truly blessed to have you in my life.

Dedication

In loving memory of my beautiful Grandmother, Shirley Cook. She was an angel on earth, taken from us too soon.

My Grandmother was the reason I started cooking at twelve years old. She always "cooked with love" and taught me to do the same. I will always remember her making the most delicious pies and hearty, satisfying dinners to fill our bellies. I would give anything to be in the kitchen with her making one of those memorable dinners one more time.

"Your life was full of loving deeds,
Forever thoughtful of our needs.
Today, tomorrow and my whole life through,
I will always love and cherish you."

Stuffed Pancakes

Ingredients

2 cups prepared pancake batter
1/2 cup pie filling or pastry cream

Directions

Prepare the pancake batter from your favorite recipe or mix. It works best if the batter is a little thinner than normal (about the thickness of cream).

Preheat a skillet or griddle by melting a little butter over medium heat. Pour an evenly round circle of pancake batter on the skillet. Let it cook until bubbles form, then pop and the indentations stay on the batter. Spoon a small amount of pastry filling on half of the pancake, making sure not to get too close to the edges and not to overfill it. A little goes a long way.

Fold the pancake over the filling. The edge of the raw batter on the top half should touch the raw batter edge on the other side when folded. It will continue to cook and seal itself on the griddle. Put a lid over the pancake to help it cook through. Flip as needed to keep the browning even.

To serve, dust the pancake with powdered sugar and fruit pancake syrup, top with whipped cream.

Serves 4.

Apple Cinnamon Pancakes

Rich, moist, fluffy pancakes that brings the decadence of apple pie to your breakfast table.

Ingredients

Pancakes

2 cups flour
1 1/2 teaspoons baking powder
1/2 teaspoon baking soda
1/2 teaspoon Kosher salt
3 tablespoons sugar
2 large eggs (yolks and whites separated)
2 1/4 cups buttermilk
4 tablespoons unsalted butter, melted and cooled
1/2 cup cinnamon chips
2 apples, thinly sliced (these will go inside the pancakes)

Apple Cinnamon Topping

4 Honeycrisp or Fuji apples, diced
6 tablespoons unsalted butter
1 cup maple syrup
1/2 teaspoon ground cinnamon
3 tablespoons brown sugar

For serving

Maple syrup or apple cider syrup

Directions

Apple cinnamon topping: heat a medium saucepan on medium heat and cook all the topping ingredients until apples have softened, about 5-10 minutes. Let cool slightly.

Mix flour, baking powder, baking soda, Kosher salt and sugar in a medium bowl.

In separate bowl, whisk egg whites with an electric mixer at medium high speed until you get stiff peaks. In a large bowl, whisk egg yolks and buttermilk. Mix in the melted butter. With a rubber spatula, fold in the egg whites until just combined.

Add the dry ingredients to the wet mixture and mix the batter, but do not overmix. It should be very lumpy and thick. Fold in cinnamon chips.

Heat electric griddle to 350 degrees for 3 minutes. Coat with butter or oil spray. Using paper towels, gently wipe any excess butter until only a thin film remains.

Pour 1/3 cup of batter for each pancake onto the griddle. Add 3 slices of apple on top of each pancake, slightly pushing them down. Cook about 2-3 minutes until you see bubbles forming on top and sides turn golden brown. Flip and cook for another 2 minutes. Repeat with the remaining batter.

To serve, stack a few pancakes and add your apple cinnamon topping and maple syrup or apple cider syrup.

Serves 6.

Blueberry Buttermilk Pancakes with Blueberry Topping

Tender, fluffy blueberry pancakes with a sweet blueberry topping.

Ingredients

Blueberry topping:

1/2 cup maple syrup
1 cup fresh blueberries
1 tablespoon lemon juice

Pancakes:

2 cups flour
2 tablespoons sugar
1 tablespoon baking powder
1/2 teaspoon baking soda
1 teaspoon salt
2 large eggs
2 1/4 cups buttermilk
4 tablespoons melted butter
1 1/2 cups fresh blueberries

Directions

Blueberry topping: Combine all ingredients in large saucepan and heat on medium low until mixture comes to a boil. Reduce heat to low and cook 10-15 minutes or until thickened. Set aside.

Pancakes: Combine all dry ingredients in a large bowl, set aside. Beat eggs in a medium bowl, whisk in buttermilk and melted butter. Pour wet ingredients slowly into the bowl of dry ingredients. Do not overmix, batter will be lumpy. Gently fold in fresh blueberries.

Heat a griddle or nonstick frying pan over medium heat. Grease with nonstick cooking spray or melted butter. Pour 1/4 cup batter on the griddle. When bubbles start to form, flip pancake and cook until golden brown.

Serve with blueberry topping and whipped cream.

Serves 6.

Double Chocolate Pancakes

For chocoholics only! This will satisfy any chocolate craving you have.

Ingredients

2 egg yolks
2 egg whites, whipped
3 tablespoons sugar
1 1/3 cups milk
3 tablespoons butter, melted
1 teaspoon vanilla extract
1 1/2 cups flour
1/4 cup cocoa powder
2 1/2 teaspoons baking powder
1/2 cup milk chocolate chips
1 tablespoon butter or oil for cooking

Directions

Whisk egg yolks and sugar in a large bowl, stir in milk. Gently fold in whipped egg whites with a rubber spatula. Add melted butter and vanilla.

In a separate bowl, mix flour, cocoa powder and baking powder. Form a well in the middle and pour the milk and egg mixture in the well. Stir until batter is smooth. Mix in chocolate chips. Let batter rest for 15-20 minutes.

Heat a griddle or nonstick frying pan over medium heat. Grease with nonstick cooking spray or melted butter. Pour 1/4 cup batter on the griddle. When bubbles start to form, flip pancake and cook until golden brown.

Serve with a drizzle of hot fudge and whipped cream. May add fresh strawberries or raspberries to top.

Puff Pancake

Ingredients

4 tablespoons butter
4 eggs
1 cup milk
1 cup flour
4 tablespoons sugar

Directions

Preheat oven to 425 degrees. Melt butter in a medium sized cast iron skillet in the oven. While butter is melting, add remaining ingredients in a medium sized bowl and whisk until well combined. This can also be done in a blender or magic bullet for even mixing.

Pour into prepared cast iron skillet and bake 18-25 minutes. Top with powdered sugar and a squeeze of fresh lemon juice or with fresh fruit.

Serves 4.

Dutch Apple Pancake With Apple Cider Syrup

Ingredients

5 tablespoons butter
2 Granny Smith apples, peeled, cored, and sliced thin
1 tablespoon cinnamon
1 cup flour
1 cup milk
1/4 teaspoon pure vanilla extract
4 eggs
1/2 cup dark brown sugar
1/2 cup sugar

Directions

In a mixing bowl, add flour, milk, vanilla and eggs. Mix well. In a separate bowl make cinnamon sugar topping by adding cinnamon and both sugars. Whisk together. Add butter to a 10 inch deep pie dish or cast iron skillet, and place in 400 degree oven. When butter is completely melted, remove from oven.

Pour batter into the pie dish and put back in the oven for 20-25 minutes. The edges will begin to puff.

Remove the half-way cooked batter from the oven and add apple mixture. Place apples over the top of the batter and cover with cinnamon sugar blend. Place back in the oven for 20-25 minutes. Remove from oven and serve hot with apple cider syrup (on following page).
Serves 2.

Apple Cider Syrup

Ingredients

½ cup brown sugar
½ cup sugar
2 tablespoons cornstarch
2 teaspoons cinnamon
⅛ teaspoon nutmeg
2 cups apple cider
2 tablespoons lemon juice
½ teaspoon vanilla
¼ cup butter

Directions

Add sugars, cinnamon, nutmeg and cornstarch to saucepan. Whisk together. Gradually add apple cider and lemon juice. Cook and whisk over medium heat until thickened to desired consistency.

Remove from heat and stir in vanilla and butter. Keep stirring until butter has melted. Drizzle over warm apple pancakes.

Makes 3 cups.

German Pancakes

A family favorite passed down from my Grandparents, to my Dad, to me. This is similar to crepes but a bit thicker.

Ingredients

2 cups flour
2 cups milk
12 eggs
1/2 teaspoon salt
2 teaspoons vanilla
4 tablespoons melted butter

Directions

Mix together first three ingredients in a large bowl. Add salt. Mix well. Add the vanilla and melted butter. Make sure mixture is not too thick.

Pour about 1/2 cup batter to cover bottom of frying pan. Cook on medium high heat in a well greased pan or skillet until lightly browned. Flip and brown the other side, another 2-3 minutes. Serve with syrup or your favorite topping.

Serves 6-8.

Basic Crepes

Ingredients

2 eggs
1 cup milk
1 cup flour
1/2 teaspoon salt
2 tablespoons butter, melted

Directions

Place all ingredients in a blender and pulse until well combined. Allow to rest 30-60 minutes.

Heat frying pan or crepe pan on medium heat and grease with butter or oil. Ladle in equal amounts of batter and tilt the pan to coat evenly. Cook until bottom is brown, flip and continue to cook about 3 minutes. Roll up with favorite fillings.

Serves 4.

Blintzes

Ingredients

Crepes

1 cup milk
1/4 cup cold water
2 eggs
1 cup flour
Pinch of salt
1 tablespoon sugar
3 tablespoons melted butter

Cheese filling

4 oz cream cheese, softened
1 cup ricotta cheese
3 tablespoons powdered sugar
1 lemon, zested
1 egg

Directions

Combine milk, water, eggs, flour, salt and sugar in a blender. Blend on medium speed 30 seconds or until lumps are gone. Add melted butter and continue to pulse for 10 seconds. Refrigerate batter for 1 hour. Remove and let rest on counter for 30 minutes.

Heat a crepe pan or nonstick skillet over medium heat and brush with melted butter or oil. Pour 1/4 cup batter in pan so it covers the entire bottom of the pan. Cook 30-45 seconds until crepe batter sets, flip and cook another 30 seconds. Slide onto a plate or platter until all crepes are ready to be rolled.
Preheat oven to 400 degrees. While oven is preheating blend all ingredients for cheese filling in a blender or food processor until smooth. Fill each crepe like a burrito, brush with butter and place in the oven for 10 minutes.

Pancake "Puffs"

If your favorite donut shop made pancakes, this would be it!

Ingredients

2 cups Krusteaz (or your favorite pancake mix)
1 cup water
Powdered sugar
Oil for frying

Optional Add-Ins (1/2 cup)

chocolate chips
dried fruit
pastry cream
jelly

If you are using an add-in, fold in the chocolate chips or dried fruit last, right before frying.

If using pastry cream or jelly, add to a piping bag with a large tip and pipe inside the pancake *after* draining on paper towels.

Directions

Mix together pancake batter. Heat oil until temperature reaches 325 degrees. Using a 1 ounce cookie scoop/ice cream scoop gently place batter into the hot oil, frying in batches about 1 minute each side, flipping only once to get both sides browned.

Drain on paper towels and dust with powdered sugar.

Makes 12 medium sized "Puffs".

Rich Buttermilk Waffles

Ingredients

3/4 cup melted butter, room temperature
3 eggs, large, separated
1 1/2 cups buttermilk
1 teaspoon vanilla extract
1 3/4 cups flour
2 teaspoons baking powder
1 teaspoon baking soda
1 tablespoon sugar
1/2 teaspoon salt

Note: bring all your cold ingredients to room temperature and it will produce an amazing waffle with better texture.

Directions

Preheat waffle iron.

In a large bowl, add all dry ingredients, stirring well to combine.

Separate eggs. Whip egg whites until stiff peaks form, set aside. Beat egg yolks and remaining liquid ingredients in a medium sized bowl. Gently fold in egg whites. Add egg mixture to dry ingredients with a wooden spoon.

Pour 1/4 cup batter into a hot, well greased waffle iron and cook until browned.

Serve with warm syrup and butter.
Makes 8-10 medium sized waffles.

Leige Waffles
(aka Europian Waffles)

These waffles have an amazing texture with a sweet sugary crunch on the top.

Ingredients

1 tablespoon active dry yeast
1 teaspoon sugar
3/4 cup whole milk warmed, 110-115 degrees
2 large eggs, room temperature, lightly beaten
4 cups bread flour
3 tablespoons packed light brown sugar
1 1/2 teaspoons salt
1 cup butter, softened
2 tablespoons honey
1 tablespoon vanilla
1 1/2 cups Belgian pearl sugar

Directions

In a stand mixer, add yeast, sugar and milk and proof yeast for 5-10 minutes. Add eggs and flour. Mix until smooth. Cover the bowl and let rise 90 minutes.

After the dough rises, add brown sugar and salt. Blend on low to medium speed. While mixing, add in honey and vanilla. Add butter, 2 tablespoons at a time. Mix 4 minutes on low to medium speed. Let dough rest for 1 minute then continue to mix for 2 minutes. Let dough rest and repeat until dough balls up on the hook.

Cover and let rest for 4 hours. Punch the dough down or use a dough hook. Wrap the dough in plastic wrap, 2-3 times around and place in a bowl. Refrigerate overnight.

The next day, place the cold dough on a slightly floured surface and knead in ALL the Belgian sugar (a little at a time). Once mixed, divide the dough into 13 equal sized pieces. Squeeze each piece into a ball and let rise for 90 minutes.

Preheat and grease waffle iron. Place 1 piece of dough into waffle iron and cook for about 4 minutes. Remove from waffle iron and serve immediately.

Makes 13 medium sized waffles.

Cinnamon Roll Waffles

Ingredients

Waffle Batter

4 eggs
1 cup sour cream
4 oz cream cheese, softened
1 cup flour
1 teaspoon vanilla
1 teaspoon baking powder
1/3 cup sugar

Cinnamon Swirl Mixture

2 tablespoons melted butter
2 tablespoons brown sugar
1 tablespoon cinnamon

Icing

4 oz cream cheese, softened
1/4 cup powdered sugar
2 tablespoons milk (or more to thin)

Directions

Preheat waffle iron. Place sour cream and cream cheese in food processor or blender and blend until smooth. Add remaining batter ingredients and pulse. Stir together ingredients for cinnamon swirl and set aside.

Spray waffle iron with nonstick cooking spray. Spoon batter on hot waffle iron and drizzle some of the cinnamon swirl mixture on top. Swirl it in gently with a toothpick, knife or spoon. Cook until golden brown. Stir together icing ingredients and set aside. Divide the icing between the waffles and serve.

Oreo Cheesecake Waffles

Ingredients

Waffles

2 cups flour

1/2 cup sugar

1 tablespoon baking powder

2 tablespoons cocoa powder

1 teaspoon salt

2 eggs

1 1/2 cups milk

8 tablespoons butter, melted

20 Oreo cookies, crushed

Cheesecake Filling

8 oz cream cheese, softened

1 cup heavy cream

1/2 cup powdered sugar

8 Oreo cookies, roughly chopped

Whipped cream for topping

Directions

Preheat waffle iron. Mix flour, sugar, baking powder, cocoa powder and salt in large bowl until well mixed. Add in eggs, milk and melted butter and stir until combined. Fold in crushed Oreos.

Grease waffle iron with nonstick cooking spray. Pour about 1/3 cup batter onto waffle iron and cook until steaming stops, about 5 minutes. Repeat with remaining batter. Set waffles aside.

For cheesecake filling, in a medium sized bowl, beat softened cream cheese until smooth. Pour in heavy cream and powdered sugar and beat until soft peaks form. Spread one waffle with cheesecake filling, then top with another waffle. (Repeat with other waffles.) Top each stack with chopped Oreos and whipped cream and serve immediately.

Birthday Cake Waffles

This is a specialty of mine. Everytime someone in our family has a birthday, I make this as their birthday breakfast. Don't forget to top with whipped cream and extra sprinkles!

Ingredients

1 box white cake mix
1/3 cup vegetable oil
1 cup water
3 large eggs
1/2 cup rainbow sprinkles, plus additional for garnish
1 cup fresh strawberries
Whipped cream

Directions

Preheat waffle iron.

Whisk cake mix, oil, water and eggs in large bowl until smooth. Stir in sprinkles. Pour 2/3 cup batter onto greased waffle iron. Cook 2 to 3 minutes or until done. Repeat with remaining batter.

Top each waffle with strawberries, whipped cream and sprinkles as desired. Serve immediately.

Makes 8-10 waffles.

Churro Waffles
With Tres Leches Sauce

Just like your favorite mexican dessert but in a delicious, fluffy waffle drizzled with a sweet sauce to top it off.

Ingredients

Waffle Batter
1 cup flour
1 teaspoon baking powder
1/4 teaspoon baking soda
1 large egg
5 tablespoons butter, melted and slightly cooled
1 cup whole milk

Cinnamon Sugar Coating
3 tablespoons melted butter
1/4 cup + 2 tablespoons sugar
1/2 tablespoon ground cinnamon

Tres Leches Sauce
1/2 cup sweetened condensed milk
1/2 cup heavy whipping cream
1/4 cup whole milk
1 teaspoon vanilla extract
1/4 teaspoon salt

Directions

Make Tres Leches sauce: In a small saucepan, combine sweetened condensed milk, heavy cream and milk. Place over medium heat and let come to a boil. Reduce heat to medium-low and simmer for 3 minutes or until thickened slightly (maintain the heat so the milk simmers, yet doesn't boil over). Take pan off heat, stir in vanilla extract and salt. Let it cool, until warm or room temperature (this sauce can be made ahead and stored at room temperature for a few hours or stored in refrigerator for 1-2 days).

For the waffles, whisk together flour, baking powder and baking soda in a medium bowl. Set aside.

In medium bowl, whisk egg, melted butter and milk until smooth. Add this wet mixture into the flour mixture and whisk to combine.

Preheat waffle iron. Spray with nonstick cooking spray. Ladle 1/3 cup batter onto the hot iron and cook waffles until golden in color.

Remove waffles and place on a wire rack (to maintain the crispness). Repeat to make remaining waffles.

Cinnamon sugar coating: Stir together sugar and ground cinnamon and place on a medium plate.

Just before serving, brush one side of each waffle with melted butter and place buttered side down on the cinnamon sugar. Press slightly for the sugar to adhere well.

Serve waffles with Tres Leches sauce on the side or drizzled on top.

Makes 8 waffles.

Bubble Waffles

Ingredients

1 cup flour
1 teaspoon baking powder
1/2 tablespoon tapioca starch
1 tablespoon custard powder
2 large eggs
2/3 cup sugar
2 tablespoons evaporated milk
5 oz water
1 tablespoon vegetable oil
1 teaspoon vanilla extract
Powdered sugar

Note: You will need a bubble waffle iron for this recipe. Bubble waffle irons can be found at any specialty kitchen store.

Directions

In a large bowl, add all ingredients and mix with a whisk until only very small lumps remain. Refrigerate one hour.

Preheat the waffle iron on medium-high heat until hot (about 1-2 minutes). Lightly brush each pan with vegetable oil (don't use spray). Turn heat to medium.

Pour 3/4 cup of the batter into the middle of the bubble waffle iron and immediately flip, making sure to hold pan together tightly so it doesn't leak. Cook for 2 minutes, then flip to other side and cook for another 2 minutes.

Remove the side of the pan the finished waffle is clinging to and hold it above a plate with the waffle upside down. Using a chopstick or spoon, gently loosen it from the pan, starting on the top edge, using gravity to help it release. It will start to curl as it falls off and should come out in one piece (except for the first waffle).

Repeat with the remaining batter (re-greasing pans first). Serve immediately. Dust with powdered sugar.

Makes 6-8 large bubble waffles.

Triple Crunch French Toast

Texas toast dipped in pancake batter, crusted with cornflakes, rolled in oats and deep fried.

Ingredients

4 thick slices of Texas Toast bread (or thick sliced brioche), cut in half
2 cups prepared pancake batter, thinned for dipping *(should be the consistency of half and half)*
1/2 cup rolled oats
1/2 cup crushed corn flakes
1 teaspoon cinnamon
1 1/2 teaspoons sugar
1 1/2 cups cooking oil to deep fat fry

Directions

Heat oil in a large frying pan on medium heat until temperature reaches 325 degrees. Cut each piece of bread in half, dip in pancake batter. If using Krusteaz, add 1/4 cup water to batter to thin out. If using homemade pancake batter, add 2 tablespoons at a time of water until pancake batter is a thinner consistency.

Stir crushed corn flakes, oats, cinnamon and sugar in a large bowl. Roll each piece of french toast in oat mixture and deep fat fry until golden brown. Serve hot with butter and maple syrup.

Serves 4

Overnight Creme Brulee French Toast

Traditional french toast with a dessert twist. When this gets baked in the oven it develops a "bruleed" topping hard to resist.

Ingredients

1/2 cup butter
5 eggs
1 teaspoon vanilla
1 cup light brown sugar
1 1/2 cups heavy whipping cream or half and half
1 loaf of Texas Toast bread (or thick sliced brioche bread)
2 tablespoons maple syrup
1/4 teaspoon salt
2 teaspoons cinnamon

Directions

In a small saucepan melt butter and brown sugar on low heat, stirring until butter has melted and mixture is smooth. Pour mixture into a lightly greased jelly roll pan (18x13) and spread out evenly on the bottom. Arrange bread slices in a single layer to cover the pan.

Add eggs to a medium bowl and beat for 1 minute, whisk in remaining ingredients. Spoon mixture evenly over bread. Cover and chill at least 8 hours or overnight.

Bake at 350 degrees 25-30 minutes or until golden brown. Flip, then broil the other side until golden brown. Serve with hot maple syrup.

Serves 4-6

Captain Crunch French Toast

Thick bread dipped in a cereal batter served with whipped cream and fresh fruit. A sweet delight!

Ingredients

4 cups Original Captain Crunch Cereal, crushed
10 slices Texas Toast bread (or thick sliced brioche bread)
4 eggs
1/2 cup heavy cream
1/2 cup sugar
1 tablespoon vanilla
1 teaspoon cinnamon
1/4 cup butter
Whipped cream and strawberries for topping

Directions

Place crushed cereal in a medium dish and set aside. Whisk eggs, cream, sugar, vanilla and cinnamon together in a shallow dish.

Melt 1 tablespoon of butter at a time in frying pan on medium heat. Dip bread in egg mixture then cereal. Fry 2-3 minutes on each side until golden brown.

Serves 6.

Hawaiian French Toast

A little taste of the islands in your home!

Ingredients

8 thick slices of brioche bread
2 large eggs
1 cup milk
1 can coconut milk
¼ cup sugar
1 teaspoon ground cinnamon
1 to 2 teaspoons coconut extract

Toppings

powdered sugar
sliced bananas
toasted coconut flakes
macadamia nuts
coconut or maple syrup
cool whip or whipped cream

Directions

Combine eggs, milks and spices in a large bowl. Soak bread in egg mixture. Melt a little butter in a large frying pan or griddle. Brown each side of the bread and place on a cookie sheet. When all the pieces are done, place cookie sheet in the oven and bake at 350° for 15 minutes. Serve with toppings of choice.

Serves 4

Strawberry Cheesecake French Toast

Ingredients

Filling

1 cup fresh strawberries, mashed
1/2 cup sugar
1 tablespoon cornstarch
1 cup cold water

French Toast

1/2 cup milk
3 large eggs
1 pinch cinnamon
1 8 oz package cream cheese, softened
1/4 cup toasted graham cracker crumbs
1 teaspoon vanilla extract
3/4 cup sugar
1 loaf thick brioche bread or Texas Toast
1 teaspoon butter

Topping

whipped cream (optional)
powdered sugar (optional)

Directions

Filling: In a medium saucepan, heat the strawberries and 1/2 cup sugar over medium heat. In a small bowl, mix cornstarch and water together and add to the strawberries. Cook and stir until thickened, about 3-5 minutes. Reduce heat to low and simmer while preparing remaining ingredients, stirring occasionally.

French toast: In a shallow bowl, whisk the eggs, milk and cinnamon together. Set aside. Mix the cream cheese, vanilla extract and 3/4 cup sugar together in a bowl until smooth. Stir in toasted graham cracker crumbs.

Make a pocket in each slice of bread. Use a spoon to stuff the cream cheese mixture into the bread. Repeat with the remaining slices of bread.

In a large skillet, heat butter over low to medium heat. Dip the stuffed bread in the egg mixture, covering both sides and letting the excess drip off, then place in the skillet. Cook until golden brown on both sides, about 3 minutes per side.

Top with strawberry syrup, whipped cream and powdered sugar. If you want a "crunchy" french toast, instead of putting the toasted graham cracker crumbs inside the french toast, double the amount of crushed graham crackers and dip each slice of bread into the graham cracker mixture after dipping it in the egg/milk mixture and pan fry it. It will give it a crispy, delicious texture on the outside.

Serves 4

Bananas Foster French Toast

A classic New Orleans dessert combined with delicious flaky croissants to make a delectable breakfast.

Ingredients

4 large eggs
1 cup heavy cream
1 teaspoon cinnamon
1 stick butter, divided
8 large croissants, halved
1/2 cup dark corn syrup
1/2 cup firmly packed brown sugar
1 cup maple syrup
1 cup toasted pecans, chopped
6 ripe bananas, sliced
1 teaspoon rum extract

Directions

In a shallow dish, whisk together eggs, cream and cinnamon. In a large skillet on medium heat melt 2 tablespoons butter.

Dip 4 croissant halves in egg mixture to coat both sides. Using a fork, remove croissants from egg mixture, letting excess drip off. Cook halves in the hot skillet. Repeat until all croissants are done. Set aside and keep warm.

In a separate large skillet, combine corn syrup, brown sugar, maple syrup and toasted pecans. Bring to a boil over medium-high heat. Once mixture comes to a boil, reduce heat to a simmer and cook an additional 2-3 minutes. Add banana slices and rum extract. Spoon over warm croissants and serve with a dollop of whipped cream and caramel sauce, if desired.

Serves 8.

Overnight Marionberry French Toast with Marionberry Syrup

Ingredients

French Toast

1 loaf French or Italian bread cut into cubes
1 cup marionberries, fresh or frozen
12 large eggs
1/2 cup **maple syrup**
2 cups half and half or heavy cream
1 tablespoon v**anilla** extract

Syrup

1 cup **sugar**
1 cup water
2 tablespoons **cornstarch**
1 cup marionberries, fresh or frozen
1 tablespoon **butter**

Directions

Arrange half of the bread cubes in a greased 9 x 13 pan. Sprinkle marionberries evenly over the bread cubes then top with remaining bread cubes. In a small bowl, mix together eggs, milk, vanilla and syrup.

Pour over bread cubes and cover pan with foil. Refrigerate overnight.

Bake covered with foil at 350 degrees for 30 minutes. Remove the foil and bake for another 30 minutes or until fluffy and golden.

While french toast is baking, whisk cornstarch in 2 tablespoons of cold water until a slurry is made.

Combine remaining ingredients in a medium saucepan and bring to a boil on medium high heat. Reduce to simmer and add cornstarch mixture. Simmer additional 5 minutes. Turn off the heat and set aside.

Remove french toast from the oven once it's golden brown and top with syrup and whipped cream.

Serves 6.

Blueberry Deluxe Muffins

Ingredients

Blueberry Muffins

2 cups flour
3 teaspoons baking powder
1/2 teaspoon salt
2 large eggs
1 cup sugar
1 cup sour cream (or yogurt)
1/2 cup canola oil
1 teaspoon vanilla extract
2 1/4 cups blueberries, fresh or frozen (thawed)
1–2 tablespoons flour

Streusel Topping

3/4 cup flour
1/4 cup sugar
1/4 cup light or dark brown sugar
6 tablespoons unsalted butter, melted

Directions

Preheat oven to 400 degrees and line standard muffin pan with liners and set aside.

Make streusel topping by blending all ingredients together with a pastry cutter or fork in a small bowl. Set aside.

For the muffins, stir together flour, baking powder and salt in a large bowl, set aside. Whisk together eggs and sugar until combined in a small bowl.

Whisk in sour cream, oil and vanilla. Fold wet ingredients into dry ingredients and mix together with a wooden spoon.

In a small bowl, sprinkle blueberries with 1-2 tablespoons flour and toss until all blueberries are coated with a thin layer of flour. Fold gently into batter. Spoon batter into prepared muffin tins, filling about 2/3 of each cup. Cover the batter generously with streusel topping.

Place in oven and reduce heat to 375 degrees. Bake about 18-20 minutes or until toothpick inserted in the center comes out clean. Allow to cool before removing from pan.

Makes 12 muffins.

Ham and Cheese Breakfast Muffins

Quick and easy breakfast on the go with plenty of protein! Change it up by adding cooked sausage or chorizo instead of bacon or ham.

Ingredients

2 eggs
3 cups Bisquick mix
1 cup buttermilk
3 tablespoons butter, melted
2 tablespoons chives
1 cup shredded pepperjack cheese
3/4 cup chopped cooked ham or bacon

Directions

Preheat oven to 400 degrees. Spray muffin tin generously with nonstick cooking spray.

Beat eggs in a large bowl, stir in Bisquick, milk and melted butter. Add chives, 3/4 cup of the cheese and ham (or bacon).

Divide batter evenly among muffin cups. Sprinkle remaining cheese over the top of the muffins and press into the batter.

Bake 18-25 minutes or until golden brown.

Makes 12 muffins.

Bran Muffins

Ingredients

4 cups Kelloggs All-Bran Buds cereal
2 cups boiling water
1 cup oil (crisco or canola)
3 cups sugar
4 eggs, beaten
1 quart buttermilk
5 cups flour
5 teaspoons baking soda
1 teaspoon salt
1 teaspoon vanilla extract
1/2 cup Sugar In The Raw, optional

Directions

Pour boiling water over the cereal in an extra large bowl. Set aside. Let stand 30 minutes to soften. Add buttermilk and vanilla. Stir well.

In a large bowl, cream sugar, oil and eggs. Add flour, soda and salt. Add to cereal mixture and stir well to combine. This mixture will keep up to 1 week in the refrigerator (I find it's best to let it sit in the refrigerator for 2-3 days before baking to enhance the flavor).

Preheat oven to 350 degrees. Spray a 12 cup muffin tin with nonstick spray and pour equal amounts into each cup, bake 8-10 minutes. If using "texas size" muffin tins, preheat oven to 325 degrees and fill 3/4 of the way full. Bake 30-35 minutes. Top with sugar in the raw (if desired) 5 minutes before removing from oven for a crunchy topping.

Makes 4 dozen regular size muffins.

Pumpkin Bran Muffins

Ingredients

2 cups bran flakes cereal
2 cups buttermilk
1 15 oz can pumpkin
1/3 cup oil
2 eggs, beaten
2 cups flour
1 1/2 cups sugar
2 teaspoons baking powder
1 teaspoon baking soda
1/2 tablespoon pumpkin pie spice

Directions

Combine cereal and buttermilk. Set aside for 30-45 minutes or until cereal is mushy. Add pumpkin, oil and eggs. Set aside for 15 minutes.

In a separate bowl, mix together flour, sugar, baking powder, baking soda and spice. Slowly stir in pumpkin mix to the dry ingredients. Stir until completely moistened.

Batter can be refrigerated for up to one week or overnight before baking (texture is better if refrigerated 1-3 days).

Spoon batter into lightly greased muffin tins, filling 3/4 of the way. Bake at 400 degrees for 18-20 minutes or until muffin tops are firm to the touch.

Makes 2 1/2 dozen muffins.

Banana Bran Muffins

Ingredients

1/2 cup oil
1/2 cup brown sugar
4 large overripe bananas
1/4 cup milk
1 teaspoon vanilla extract
2 eggs
1 1/2 cups flour
1/2 cup wheat bran
1 teaspoon baking powder
1 teaspoon baking soda
1/4 teaspoon salt
1/2 cup chocolate chips (optional)

Directions

Preheat oven to 375 degrees. Grease muffin tins.

In a large mixing bowl, cream oil and sugar until fluffy. Add bananas, milk, vanilla and eggs. Mix well. Stir in remaining ingredients.

Pour batter into prepared muffin tins, filling 3/4 of the way. Bake 20-25 minutes.

Makes a dozen muffins.

Apple Bran Muffins

Apple cinnamon goodness in every bite.

Ingredients

1 1/2 cups bran cereal
1 cup flour
1 cup milk
1/3 cup applesauce
1 egg
1 teaspoon baking soda
1 teaspoon baking powder
2/3 cup brown sugar
1/2 teaspoon vanilla
1/2 tablespoon cinnamon
2 large apples, peeled, cored and diced (optional)
1 cup cinnamon chips (optional)

Directions

Mix all ingredients together in a large bowl and set aside for 45 minutes.

Pour 3/4 cup batter into well greased muffin tins.

Bake at 375 degrees for 15-20 minutes.

Makes 1 dozen muffins.

Basic Cream Scones

You can't go wrong with this basic scone recipe for tea time. Add your favorite dried fruit to these and serve with fresh lemon curd and devonshire or clotted cream.

Ingredients

1 3/4 cups flour
4 teaspoons baking powder
1/4 cup sugar
1/8 teaspoon salt
5 tablespoons unsalted butter
1/2 cup milk
1/4 cup sour cream
1 egg
1 tablespoon milk

Optional add-ins:

Add a total of 1/2 cup to the batter:

white chocolate chips and raspberries
dried cherries and dark/milk chocolate chips
fresh blueberries with 1 tablespoon lemon zest
chopped apples, peeled and tossed with 1 tablespoon cinnamon sugar
fresh strawberries, top baked scones with powdered sugar glaze
shredded coconut with 1 tablespoon lime zest and 2 tablespoons lime juice

Directions

Preheat oven to 400 degrees. Sift all dry ingredients together in a large bowl. Cut butter in with a pastry cutter until it looks like pea sized lumps. Stir in optional add ins. Make a well in the middle of the flour mixture and slowly pour in milk and fold in sour cream. Mix gently. Do not over work the dough.

With floured hands, pat scone dough into an 8-9 inch disc. Cut into 8 wedges, separate and place on well greased cookie sheet or parchment lined baking sheet at least 1 inch apart. Whisk together egg and 1 tablespoon milk. Brush scones with the egg wash and top with raw sugar, if desired. Let rest 10 minutes.

Bake 10-15 minutes or until tops are golden brown. Serve with butter or clotted cream and lemon curd.

Makes 8 scones.

Don't have a pastry cutter? Here is a little tip.... freeze your butter in advance and shred it! Cut it into your scones with a fork or use your hands to mix the dough until it resembles coarse sand like texture.

Triple Chocolate Scones
A delicious tender scone perfect for chocolate lovers.

Ingredients
1 2/3 cups flour
1/3 cup unsweetened cocoa powder
1/2 cup sugar
2 1/2 teaspoons baking powder
1/2 teaspoon ground cinnamon
1/2 teaspoon salt
1/2 cup unsalted butter, frozen
1/2 cup + 1 tablespoon heavy cream
1 large egg
1 1/2 teaspoons vanilla extract
6 oz milk chocolate chips

Glaze
1 cup powdered sugar
1 teaspoon vanilla extract
2 tablespoons water (black coffee works too!)
4 oz semi-sweet chocolate, coarsely chopped

Directions

Preheat oven to 400 degrees. Adjust baking rack to the middle position of the oven.

Line a large baking sheet with parchment paper or a silicone baking mat. Set aside.

In a large bowl, whisk flour, cocoa, sugar, baking powder, cinnamon and salt. Grate the frozen butter and toss into flour mixture. Using a pastry cutter or two knives cut the butter in until the mixture resembles coarse meal. Set aside.

In a small bowl, whisk the cream, egg and vanilla together. Drizzle over flour mixture and stir with a rubber spatula until moistened. Add more heavy cream, 1 teaspoon at a time, until it comes together, if needed. Gently fold in the chopped chocolate. Do not overwork the dough.

Transfer to the prepared baking sheet. Press into a neat 8 inch disc and cut into 8 equal wedges with a very sharp knife. Separate the scones and line them on the baking sheet with a little space between each one.

Bake for 20-25 minutes or until cooked through; use a toothpick to check if it's done. A toothpick inserted will come out mostly clean. Remove scones from the oven and allow to cool for a couple minutes.

While scones are baking, prepare glaze by whisking powdered sugar, vanilla and water together until smooth and thin. Dunk warm scones into the glaze and place on a wire rack with a baking sheet or paper towels underneath to catch the glaze. The glaze will set after several minutes.

Before serving, melt 4 ounces of semi-sweet chocolate in the microwave in 15 second increments, stirring after each increment until melted. Drizzle over scones.

Makes 8 scones.

Jalapeno Bacon Cheese Scones

A cheesy, spicy scone with crispy pepper bacon in the mix.

Ingredients

2 cups flour
1/2 teaspoon salt
1 tablespoon baking powder
6 tablespoons cold butter cut into small pieces
1 cup cheddar cheese, grated
2 strips cooked pepper bacon, chopped
3 stalks scallions, chopped (both white and green parts)
1/4 cup jalapenos, diced
2 large eggs
1/3 cup sour cream

Directions

Preheat oven to 375 degrees. Line a baking sheet with parchment paper. In a large mixing bowl whisk together flour, salt and baking powder. Add the pieces of cold butter using a pastry cutter. The mixture should turn into coarse meal.

Add cheese, jalapenos, bacon and scallions in a separate bowl. Stir in sour cream and eggs. Add wet mixture to dry ingredients and stir until batter is sticky. Do not overmix. Place dough on a floured surface. Pat scone dough into a 8-9 inch disc. Cut into 8 wedges.

Place on baking sheet with about an inch of space in between. Bake at 375 degrees for 16-20 minutes or until the scones are lightly golden. Store in a tightly covered container at room temperature.
Makes 8 scones.

Apple Sour Cream Coffee Cake

Delicious coffee cake with a sweet cinnamon apple filling.

Ingredients

Cake

1/2 cup butter, softened
1 cup sugar
2 large eggs
2 cups flour, sifted
1 teaspoon baking soda
1 teaspoon baking powder
1/2 teaspoon salt
1 1/2 cups sour cream
1 teaspoon vanilla extract
2 large Gala apples, peeled, cored and sliced

Topping

1/3 cup light brown sugar
1/4 cup sugar
1 teaspoon ground cinnamon

Directions

Topping

Combine all the ingredients and mix well. Set aside.

Coffee Cake

Heat oven to 325 degrees. Lightly coat an 8X8 baking pan with nonstick cooking spray.

With a hand mixer, cream butter, sugar and eggs in a large bowl until smooth. Add flour, baking soda, baking powder, salt, sour cream and vanilla, mix well. Fold in apples. Pour batter in prepared dish.

Bake for 1 hour or until toothpick inserted comes out clean. Refrigerate 1 hour before serving.

10-12 servings.

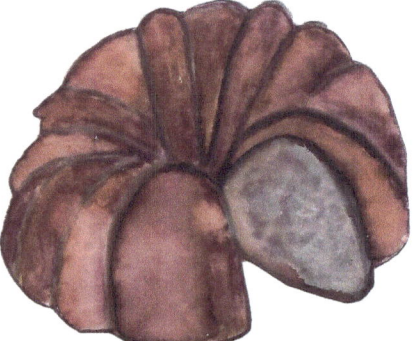

Lemon Coffee Cake

Tart, creamy lemon curd adds a bright tang to this coffee cake.

Ingredients

Crumb Topping

2/3 cup flour
dash of salt
3 tablespoons light brown sugar
5 tablespoons sugar
4 tablespoons unsalted butter, melted and slightly cooled

Cake

1 ½ cups flour
1 teaspoon baking powder
¼ teaspoon salt
6 tablespoons unsalted butter, softened
1 cup sugar
1 teaspoon vanilla
1 large lemon, zested
2 eggs
¾ cup sour cream
1 cup lemon curd (store bought or homemade)
powdered sugar (if desired)

Lemon Curd

½ cup lemon juice
2 teaspoons lemon zest
½ cup sugar
2 eggs
5 tablespoons unsalted butter

Directions

Lemon Curd:

In a saucepan melt the butter. Remove from heat. Add sugar, lemon juice and lemon zest, whisk to combine. Add eggs and whisk well. Place over medium heat and cook for 5-6 minutes until all the sugar is dissolved and mixture is thick enough to coat the back of a spoon. Cool completely.

Cake:

Preheat oven to 350 degrees. Line 8x8x2 inch square baking pan (or 9x9 inch pan) with parchment paper leaving an overhang on the sides, coat with nonstick cooking spray and set aside.

Make crumb topping. In a small bowl, stir together flour, sugar, brown sugar and salt. Add melted butter and stir with a fork until pea size crumbs form. Refrigerate until ready to use.

For the cake, in a large bowl beat softened butter for one minute, add sugar and beat until creamy. Add lemon zest, vanilla and eggs and mix to combine. Fold in sour cream and mix well. Add flour, baking powder and salt. Spread half of the batter in prepared pan.

Spread 1 cup of lemon curd over the batter but don't go all the way to the edges (or it will burn during baking). Spoon remaining batter on top. Sprinkle with crumb topping and bake about 45-55 minutes or until the center has set. If it browns too quickly, tent the top with aluminum foil.

Cool for 30 minutes in the pan, then pull the paper and lift the cake out to transfer to a rack and cool completely. Dust with powdered sugar before serving.

Serves 8-10.

Marionberry Coffee Cake

Ingredients

1 cup flour
6 tablespoons sugar
1 1/2 teaspoons baking powder
1/4 teaspoon baking soda
1/8 teaspoon salt
2 tablespoons butter, melted
1 large egg
1/2 cup buttermilk
3/4 teaspoon vanilla

Crumb topping

2 tablespoons flour
1 tablespoon sugar
1 tablespoon melted butter
1/4 teaspoon vanilla extract
generous pinch of cinnamon

Berry reduction

2/3 cup fresh or frozen marionberries
1 tablespoon water
1 teaspoon cornstarch
1 tablespoon sugar
1/2 tablespoon lemon juice

Directions

Berry Reduction

Mix berries, cornstarch, water, lemon juice and sugar together in a medium sized bowl and microwave in small increments until they are slightly thickened, stirring often.

Crumb Topping

Mix all the topping ingredients together until well combined and a crumbly mixture forms.

Cake

Preheat oven to 350 degrees. Line an 8 inch square pan with parchment paper overhanging on the sides or spray pan liberally with nonstick cooking spray before pouring in batter for easy removal. Set aside.

Sift flour, baking powder, baking soda and salt together in a medium mixing bowl, set aside. Mix egg, sugar, melted butter, vanilla and buttermilk together in a small bowl. Pour the wet ingredients over flour mixture and fold until combined.

Layer the pan with half of the cake mixture. Make second layer using half of the marionberry reduction. Pour the remaining batter in pan. Top batter with remaining berry reduction and finish with crumb topping.

Bake for 25-35 minutes or until the cake springs back when touched.

Allow cake to cool for 30-60 minutes before serving.

Serves 8-10.

Better Than "Drakes" Mini Coffee Cakes

Ingredients

Cake

2 large eggs
1 cup whole milk
3 cups flour
1 1/2 cups sugar
4 teaspoons baking powder
1/2 teaspoon salt
1 cup butter, melted

Crumb Topping

2 1/2 cups flour
2 cups sugar
2 tablespoons ground cinnamon
1 cup butter, melted
2 teaspoons vanilla extract

Directions

Cake

Preheat oven to 350 degrees. Spray a mini loaf baking pan (usually makes 8 mini loaves) or a 12 cup muffin tin with nonstick spray.

Whisk eggs and milk in a medium sized bowl, set aside.

Combine all dry ingredients together then slowly whisk in melted butter. Add egg mixture and whisk gently until well combined.

Pour batter into the prepared pan. Make the topping.

Topping

Combine dry ingredients in a small bowl and stir with a fork to combine. Add butter and vanilla and mix well until crumbly. Press gently on top of the coffee cake batter.

For muffin tins, bake 25-30 minutes. **(Serves 12)**
For mini loaves, bake 30-35 minutes. **(Serves 8)**

Apple Cinnamon Danish

Ingredients

1 tube crescent rolls
1 (20 oz) can apple pie filling
2 tablespoons butter, melted
cinnamon sugar
1/2 cup powdered sugar
1 teaspoon vanilla extract
3-4 teaspoons milk

Directions

Preheat oven to 350 degrees. Separate dough into eight rectangles. Using a brush or spoon, spread melted butter over crescent rolls. Sprinkle with cinnamon sugar mixture (2 tablespoons sugar mixed with 1 teaspoon of cinnamon). Reserve 1 tablespoon. Roll up from long side and pinch edges to seal. Holding one end, loosely coil each roll. Spread out the dough in the center to make room for the filling.

Place on cookie sheet that has been sprayed with nonstick spray. Open can of apple pie filling and using a knife, cut apple slices into smaller chunks. Top each coil with about 2-3 tablespoons of apple pie filling. Sprinkle the tops with a bit more cinnamon sugar mixture.

Bake at 350 degrees for 15-18 minutes or until golden brown. For the glaze, combine all ingredients in a small bowl and stir until smooth. Drizzle over warm danishes.

Serves 8.

Fruit & Cream Cheese Danish

Ingredients

1 box puff pastry dough (2 sheets), thawed
1 8 oz package cream cheese
1 tablespoon sour cream
3 tablespoons sugar
2 teaspoons lemon juice
lemon zest from one lemon
2 1/2 teaspoons vanilla extract
fresh blueberries, rinsed and dried
fresh strawberries, stems removed and cut in half
3 tablespoons melted butter, for brushing
Sanding sugar

Directions

Adjust oven rack to center position. Preheat oven to 400 degrees.

Unfold the thawed puff pastry sheets on a lightly-floured board. With a large 4.5-inch biscuit cutter, cut out 4 rounds of dough from each piece. Lightly score the rounds with a slightly-smaller biscuit cutter or drinking glass.

Transfer the puff pastry rounds to baking sheets lined with silicone baking mats or parchment paper. Gather together the remaining scraps of dough. Roll out the dough and create two or three more danish pastry circles. Add those to the baking sheets.

In a stand mixer bowl, add cream cheese, sour cream, sugar, lime juice, lime zest and vanilla extract. Mix until all ingredients are fully incorporated and the consistency is smooth and creamy. Place two tablespoons of the cream cheese mixture in the center of each puff pastry circle. Using the backside of a spoon, spread it out leaving a 1/4-inch rim.

Arrange blueberries on half of the rounds. Artistically arrange strawberries on the rest of the batch.

Bake for 15-16 minutes or until the rims of the puff pastry desserts are lightly golden brown. Allow the cheese danish to cool for about 15 minutes.

Makes 8 danishes.

Banana Walnut Bread

Ingredients

1 1/2 cups flour
1/2 teaspoon salt
1/2 teaspoon baking powder
1/2 teaspoon baking soda
1 1/2 teaspoons cinnamon
1 cup sugar
1 large egg
1/2 cup canola oil
2 teaspoons vanilla extract
1 cup mashed, overripe bananas
2/3 cup chopped walnuts

Icing

1 cup powdered sugar
1/2 teaspoon vanilla extract
1/4 cup milk (or more to thin icing to your taste)

Directions

Preheat oven to 325 degrees. Spray and line a 9x5 loaf pan with parchment paper and set aside.

Whisk all dry ingredients together in a large mixing bowl. Beat in wet ingredients with hand mixer. Fold in nuts last. Pour into pan and bake 60-75 minutes until toothpick inserted comes out clean. Remove from oven and cool completely.

Beat sugar, vanilla and milk in a small bowl until icing is smooth. Spread over cooled bread.

Lemon Loaf

Ingredients

3 eggs
1 cup sugar
1 cup sour cream
1/2 cup vegetable oil
2 tablespoons lemon zest
2 tablespoons lemon extract
1 1/2 cups flour
2 teaspoons baking powder
1/2 teaspoon salt

Lemon Glaze
2-3 tablespoons fresh lemon juice
1 cup powdered sugar

Directions

Preheat oven to 350 degrees. Spray a 9x5 loaf pan with nonstick cooking spray and set aside.

In a large bowl, add eggs, sugar, sour cream and oil and mix well by hand until smooth. Add lemon extract and lemon zest, stir well until combined.

In a small bowl whisk together remaining dry ingredients then stir into egg mixture. Pour batter into loaf pan and bake 60-75 minutes or until toothpick inserted comes out clean. Cool completely.

Using a hand mixer or whisk, beat glaze ingredients until smooth. Frost lemon loaf, once cooled.
Serves 6-8.

Apple Fritter Loaf

Ingredients

1/3 cup brown sugar
1/2 tablespoon cinnamon
2 large apples of any kind, peeled and diced
1 stick unsalted butter
2/3 cup sugar
1 1/2 teaspoons vanilla extract
1 1/2 cups flour
1 3/4 teaspoons baking soda

For the glaze

1/2 cup powdered sugar
1/4 cup milk or heavy cream (add more to thin, if desired)

Directions

Preheat oven to 350 degrees. Generously grease 9x5 loaf pan with nonstick cooking spray and set aside.

In a small mixing bowl, add apples, brown sugar and cinnamon. Toss well to combine. Set aside.

In a medium sized bowl, with a hand mixer, beat butter and sugar together until creamy. Add eggs and vanilla extract, mix until well combined. Stir in milk, baking soda and flour. Pour half of the batter into the prepared loaf pan. Place half of the apple mixture on top of the batter and press gently into the dough. Add remaining batter on top and finish with remaining apples, pressing gently into the dough.

Bake 1 hour or until toothpick inserted comes out clean. Remove from oven and cool completely. Mix glaze ingredients into a small bowl until smooth. Spoon glaze over cooled bread.

Pumpkin Bread with Maple Butter Icing

Ingredients

Pumpkin Bread

1/2 cup butter, softened
1 cup light brown sugar
1 cup canned pumpkin puree
2 eggs
1 1/2 teaspoons ground cinnamon
1/2 tablespoon pumpkin pie spice
1 teaspoon baking powder
1 teaspoon baking soda
1 teaspoon salt
1 1/2 cups flour

Maple Butter Icing

1/2 cup butter
1 1/2 cups powdered sugar
1-2 tablespoons maple syrup
2 tablespoons milk

Directions

Preheat oven to 350 degrees. Spray a 9x5 loaf pan generously with nonstick cooking spray.

Combine all bread ingredients in a large bowl and beat at medium speed with a hand held mixer, scraping down the sides of the bowl, until well combined.

Pour the bread mixture into the prepared pan. Bake for one hour or until a toothpick inserted near the center comes out clean.

While cooling, make your glaze. In a small saucepan, heat butter over medium-low heat until melted. Continue cooking, watching butter carefully, until it starts to turn light brown in color, about 4-5 minutes.

When butter looks caramel-colored, it's done. Remove butter from heat and cool completely. Stir in powdered sugar and maple syrup until a soft glaze has formed. Stir in milk. Pour glaze over top of the pumpkin loaf and let set 30-45 minutes.

Serves 6-8.

Easy Chocolate Croissants

Tastes just like the fancy ones from your favorite coffee shop.

Ingredients

8 croissants
1 1/2 cups milk chocolate chips
3 tablespoons pure maple syrup
¼ cup raw coarse sugar

Directions

Preheat oven to 425 degrees and line a baking sheet with foil or parchment paper.

Cut each croissant in-half horizontally, but not all the way through. Place each croissant on the baking sheet and evenly divide up chocolate chips between the 8 croissants. Close the top of each croissant and lightly brush the tops with maple syrup. Sprinkle with coarse or raw sugar.

Place the baking sheet in the oven on the lowest rack and bake for 4-5 minutes or until the tops are golden brown and have caramelized. Watch the croissants closely beginning at 4 minutes. They can burn quickly at this point.
Transfer the croissants to a cooling rack and cool for 1 minute. These are delicious warm or cold.

Makes 8.

Pudding Filled Donut Holes

Ingredients

1 container Pillsbury Flaky Layers Biscuits
1 small box pudding mix (any flavor, jelly or pastry cream can be used also)
1 cup powdered sugar
Oil for frying

Directions

Separate biscuits and cut each one into 4 pieces, rolling each one into little balls.

Heat 2" of oil in a deep skillet or deep fat fryer until the temperature reaches 350 degrees.

Make pudding according to package directions. Refrigerate for 2-3 hours. Add to a piping bag and set aside.

Drop 4 donut holes in at a time, cooking until golden brown, about 1-2 minutes. Drain on paper towels.

In a small paper lunch bag, add powdered sugar. Toss warm donut holes in the bag until well coated.

Gently pipe in jelly or pudding filling. Serve immediately.

Makes about 32 donut holes.

Cronuts

In case you missed the "cronut craze" here is a quick and easy way to make your own at home.

Ingredients

1 tube crescent rolls or thawed puff pastry dough
1 cup powdered sugar
2-3 teaspoons water or milk
Cinnamon sugar
Oil for frying (Canola is best, but you can use vegetable or peanut oil)

Directions

Remove dough from the package. Layer each piece of dough before cutting it into donuts. This is how you get all those layers in a cronut. You will only get 3-6 donuts total after all the layering.

On medium heat, add enough oil in a deep skillet or cast iron pot to come up half way. Heat to 350 degrees.

If using puff pastry dough, you will need to fry it for about 45-50 seconds on each side. For the crescent roll dough, only about 30 seconds on each side. After frying, remove the cronuts to a plate lined with paper towels to soak up excess grease. Toss warm cronuts in cinnamon sugar.

For the glaze, add 1 cup powdered sugar and 1 tablespoon water (or milk) in a medium size bowl and mix until smooth. Dip each cronut into glaze.

Makes 3-6 donuts.

Mom's Best Donuts

I remember as a little girl looking forward to winter just to wake up to the smell of these delightful donuts. My Mom would fix hot chocolate for my brother and I and when the donuts would come out of the fryer, we would put them in a paper bag and shake them up with powdered sugar.

Ingredients

3 1/3 cups flour
1 cup sugar
3 teaspoons baking powder
1/2 teaspoon salt
1/2 teaspoon cinnamon
1/4 teaspoon nutmeg
2 tablespoons shortening
2 eggs
3/4 cup milk
oil for frying
powdered sugar

Directions

Heat 2-3 inches of oil in a deep fat fryer or heavy kettle to 375 degrees.

Beat 1 1/2 cups flour and remaining ingredients in a large bowl on low speed scraping bowl as you mix. Beat on medium speed for additional 2-3 minutes. Stir in remaining flour.

Turn dough onto a well floured surface, roll around lightly to coat with flour. Roll dough 3/8 inch thick. Cut with floured donut cutter, use scraps for donut holes. Gently drop donuts into hot oil. Turn donuts as they rise to the top surface. Fry 1 1/2 minutes or until golden brown. Remove from oil and drain on paper towel lined baking sheet.
Place 2 cups powdered sugar in a doubled up, lunch sized paper bag. Add a few hot donuts at a time, tossing to coat evenly.
Makes 2 Dozen Donuts.

Simple Cinnamon Rolls

Dough

1 lb. frozen bread loaf, defrosted
3 tablespoons butter
1/2 cup brown sugar
1 1/2 teaspoons ground cinnamon
1/3 cup heavy cream

Cream Cheese Frosting

8 oz cream cheese, softened
2/3 cup sifted powdered sugar
2 tablespoons milk, or more as needed
1 teaspoon vanilla extract

Directions

Preheat oven to 350 degrees. Sprinkle work surface with flour. Roll out defrosted bread loaf into a long rectangle. Spread melted butter on top of dough followed by brown sugar and cinnamon.

Start from the longer end and roll up dough. Cut into 12 equal sized rolls. Brush heavy cream on top. Place rolls into a well greased cake pan or casserole pan. Cover rolls and let rise until they double in size (about 1 1/2 hours).

Bake at 350 degrees for 25 minutes.

For cream cheese frosting, beat all ingredients in a large mixing bowl until glaze is smooth. Add milk to get desired thickness. Spread over rolls.

Caramel Pecan Sticky Buns

Ingredients

1 1/4 cups powdered sugar
1/3 cup heavy whipping cream
1 cup toasted pecans, chopped
1/2 cup brown sugar
1 tablespoon cinnamon
2 frozen white bread dough loaves, thawed
3 tablespoons butter, melted

Directions

Grease a 9x13 pan with cooking spray.

In a small bowl, combine powdered sugar and heavy whipping cream. Pour into prepared pan. Sprinkle toasted pecans over the top and set aside. Combine brown sugar and cinnamon in small bowl, set aside.

On a lightly floured surface, roll out one bread loaf into a rectangle (roughly the same size as the 9x13 pan). Pour half of the butter onto the dough and spread it out. Sprinkle half of the cinnamon/sugar mixture over the butter.

Roll up the dough from the longer side of the rectangle shape and cut dough roll into 8 pieces. Place each slice in the pan on top of the pecans. Place 4 cinnamon rolls in each row. Repeat with second loaf.

Cover with plastic wrap that has been sprayed with nonstick cooking spray. Leave in refrigerator overnight. Set covered rolls out at room temperature for 1 hour before baking. Bake at 350 degrees for 25-30 minutes. Let cool on wire rack for 5 minutes. Turn pan upside down on a serving platter. Serve warm.

Makes 16 rolls.

SECTION 3
Skillet Breakfasts and Omelets

Yorkshire "Pirate Eyes"

An English style breakfast with a traditional yorkshire pudding base and delicious sausage patties nestled in.

Ingredients

3 large eggs
1 cup milk
1/2 teaspoon salt
1 cup flour
12 ounces uncooked sausage patties
3 tablespoons butter
maple syrup, optional

Directions

Preheat oven to 400 degrees. In a small bowl, whisk eggs, milk and salt. Whisk flour into egg mixture until blended. Let stand 30 minutes. Cook sausage according to package directions, set aside.

Place butter in a 12-inch nonstick ovenproof skillet. Place in oven until melted, 3-4 minutes. Stir batter and pour into prepared skillet; top with sausage. Bake until golden brown and puffed, 20-25 minutes. Remove from skillet. Cut into wedges. If desired, serve with butter and syrup.

Serves 6.

Breakfast Pizza

A crispy hashbrown crust with your favorite breakfast toppings.

Ingredients

1 pound bulk breakfast sausage (can substitute for bacon or ham)

5 cups frozen shredded hash brown potatoes

1/2 cup chopped onion

1/4 cup chopped red bell pepper

1/4 to 1/2 teaspoon salt

Pepper to taste

1/2 cup sliced mushrooms

2 tablespoons diced jalapeno

1 medium size beefsteak tomato, diced

4 large eggs, lightly beaten

1 cup shredded sharp cheddar cheese

Sour cream and salsa, optional

Directions

Preheat oven to 400 degrees. Grease a medium sized cast iron skillet generously with nonstick cooking spray. Press hashbrowns into cast iron skillet to form a "crust". Bake 20-25 minutes until golden brown, remove from oven.

In a large skillet, cook sausage over medium heat until no longer pink. Add the onion, red bell pepper, jalapeno, salt and pepper. Cook on medium low heat until onions and peppers are soft, about 5-7 minutes. Add mushrooms and cook an additional 5 minutes. Remove from heat. Sprinkle sausage mixture over hashbrown "crust", pour eggs over the potato mixture. Arrange diced tomatoes on top. Sprinkle with cheese.

Cover and cook over medium-low heat for 10-15 minutes or until eggs are completely set (do not stir).

Serve with sour cream and salsa if desired.

Serves 6

Creamy Egg & Bacon Au Gratin

A creamy egg base with cheesy au gratin sauce.

Ingredients

2 tablespoons butter

1 pound chopped, cooked thick pepper bacon

1 green onion, chopped

Sauce

2 tablespoons butter, melted

3 tablespoons flour

1/2 teaspoon salt

1/8 teaspoon pepper

1 cup milk

1/2 cup heavy whipping cream

2 tablespoons grated parmesan cheese

Eggs

16 large eggs

1/4 teaspoon salt

1/8 teaspoon pepper

1/4 cup butter, cubed

1/2 cup grated parmesan cheese

1 green onion, finely chopped

Directions

Preheat broiler.

In a large broiler-safe skillet, heat butter over medium-high heat. Add mushrooms; cook and stir until browned, about 4-6 minutes. Add green onion and cook for 1 minute. Remove from pan with a slotted spoon. Clean skillet and set aside.

For sauce: melt butter over medium heat in a small saucepan. Whisk in flour, salt and pepper until smooth. Gradually whisk in milk and cream. Bring to a boil, stirring constantly. Cook and stir until thickened, 2-4 minutes. Remove from heat and stir in cheese.

For eggs: in a large bowl, whisk eggs, salt and pepper until blended. Add butter to skillet, melt over medium heat. Pour in egg mixture. Cook and stir just until eggs are thickened and no liquid egg remains. Remove from heat.

Spoon half of the sauce over the eggs and top with bacon. Add remaining sauce and sprinkle with cheese. Broil 4-5 inches from heat until top is lightly browned, 4-6 minutes. Sprinkle with green onion.

Serves 4-6.

Garden Fresh Frittata

Ingredients

2 small potatoes, peeled and cut into 1/2-inch cubes

8 large eggs, lightly beaten

2 tablespoons heavy cream

1/4 teaspoon salt

1/8 teaspoon garlic powder

1/8 teaspoon chili powder

1/8 teaspoon pepper

1 small zucchini, chopped

1/4 cup chopped onion

2 tablespoons fresh chives, diced

1 tablespoon butter

1 tablespoon olive oil

1 large beefsteak tomato, sliced thin

8 oz goat cheese or cheddar cheese, shredded

Directions

Preheat oven to 425 degrees.

Place potatoes in a small saucepan and cover with water. Bring to a boil. Reduce heat; cover and simmer 5 minutes. Drain.

In a large bowl, whisk eggs, cream, salt, garlic powder, chili powder and pepper, set aside.

In a 10-inch cast-iron or ovenproof skillet, saute zucchini, onion and potatoes in butter and oil until tender. Reduce heat. Pour 1 1/2 cups egg mixture into skillet. Arrange half of the tomatoes over top; sprinkle with half of the cheese. Top with remaining egg mixture, tomatoes and cheese.

Bake uncovered until eggs are completely set, 12-15 minutes. Let stand 5 minutes. Sprinkle with chives and additional cheese. Cut into wedges.

Serves 2.

Mediterranean Omelet

Ingredients

8 oz cherry tomatoes, diced

1/2 medium sized zucchini, cubed

1 small yellow onion, diced

1 small red pepper, diced

6 large eggs

1/4 cup 2% milk

1/2 teaspoon salt

1/4 teaspoon pepper

1/2 teaspoon greek oregano

1/3 cup crumbled feta

1/3 cup sliced pitted Greek olives

4 tablespoons olive oil

fresh parsley to top

Directions

Heat a large oven safe skillet on medium heat. Add all vegetables to the pan except diced tomato. Drizzle olive oil over the top and stir until well combined. Cook for 7-10 minutes or until vegetables are tender.

In a large bowl, whisk eggs, milk, salt and pepper. Stir in cheese and olives. Add egg mixture to the pan. Cook uncovered 4-6 minutes or until nearly set. Broil 3-4 inches from heat for 2-4 minutes or until eggs are completely set. Remove from oven and cool 5-7 minutes. Cut into wedges.

Top with fresh parsley and tomato.

Ham, Chile and Cheese Baked Omelet

A cheesy, slightly spicy omelet easily put together in less than 10 minutes!

Ingredients

2 1/2 cups shredded cheddar cheese, divided
2 4 oz cans diced fire roasted green chiles
1 16 oz package diced ham
8 eggs
1 12 oz can fat free evaporated milk
salt and pepper to taste
dried parsley

Directions

Grease a 9x13 inch baking dish with cooking spray. Combine 2 cups shredded cheese with green chiles. Spoon mixture evenly over the bottom of the prepared baking dish. Sprinkle the diced ham on top of the chile-cheese mixture.

Whisk eggs and milk in a medium bowl and season with salt and pepper. Pour evenly over ingredients in the baking dish. Sprinkle the top with remaining 1/2 cup shredded cheese and dried parsley. Cover dish with foil and bake at 375 degrees for 60 minutes, removing the foil for the last 15 minutes to slightly brown the top.

Serves 2.

Traditional French Omelet

Ingredients

3 eggs, whipped

1 tablespoon unsalted butter

Optional fillings

1/4 cup shredded cheese,

2 tablespoons diced ham or bacon

1/4 cup sauteed vegetables

Directions

Heat nonstick frying pan over medium heat and melt butter, tipping the pan so the bottom of the frying pan is coated.

Add whipped eggs, constantly stirring with a spatula. As eggs begin to set up they will start to pull away from the sides and bottom of the pan. When eggs are almost done cooking add your fillings in a straight line across the bottom side of the omelet. Using a rubber spatula gently pull up the sides of the omelet to seal the filling. Continue to roll the omelet until it is folded in thirds. Serve warm.

Serves 1.

Country Skillet

Ingredients

6 thick cut slices of bacon

6 cups frozen, cubed, hash brown potatoes

1/4 cup chopped green pepper

1/4 cup chopped red pepper

1/2 cup diced onion

1 teaspoon salt

1/4 teaspoon pepper

6 large eggs

1/2 cup shredded sharp cheddar cheese

Directions

In a large skillet over medium heat, cook bacon until crisp. Remove bacon; crumble and set aside. Drain, reserving 2 tablespoons of drippings. Add the potatoes, peppers, onion, salt and pepper to drippings; cook and stir for 2 minutes. Cover and cook for about 15 minutes or until potatoes are browned and tender, stirring occasionally.

Make six wells in the potato mixture; break one egg into each well. Cover and cook on low heat for 8-10 minutes or until eggs are completely set. Sprinkle with cheese and bacon.

SECTION 4
Quiche & Benedicts

Classic Eggs Benedict

An easier approach to the classic dish, with some fun variations.

Ingredients
Hollandaise

3 large egg yolks
1/4 teaspoon Dijon mustard
1 tablespoon lemon juice
1/2 teaspoon Tabasco sauce
1/2 cup unsalted butter, melted
Kosher salt to taste

Benedict

8 poached eggs
8 english muffins, toasted
8 oz canadian bacon or ham, sliced or shaved

Directions

Prepare poached eggs the easy way: Heat oven to 350 degrees. Using a lightly greased 12 cup muffin tin, pour 1 tablespoon water in each cup. Crack egg over each cup and bake 8-10 minutes. Use a slotted spoon to scoop eggs out gently.

Preheat oven to 200 degrees. Lightly toast english muffins. Arrange on baking sheet, top with equal portions of canadian bacon or ham. Allow to stay warm in the oven. Stack egg on top of english muffins equally to keep warm.

To make hollandaise: add egg yolks, Dijon mustard, lemon juice and Tabasco sauce to a blender. Blend for 5 seconds to combine. Slowly pour in melted butter in a slow steady stream into the blender and blend as you are pouring it in. The sauce should thicken immediately. Add salt if desired. Spoon equal portions of hollandaise over each egg. Garnish with minced chives and parsley. Serve immediately.

Florentine Benedict

Ingredients

1 large beefsteak tomato, sliced
1 teaspoon extra virgin olive oil
1 5 oz container spinach
1/4 teaspoon kosher salt
1/8 teaspoon freshly ground black pepper
1/4 teaspoon ground nutmeg
4 sourdough english muffins, toasted

Directions

Toast english muffins and set aside. Place a thick slice of tomato on each muffin. Broil under medium heat for 3-5 minutes to soften tomato. Remove from oven and set aside.

In a large skillet, warm olive oil over medium-high heat. Add spinach to skillet and cook for 3 minutes or until spinach is wilted. Mix in salt, ground pepper and nutmeg. Evenly divide spinach and place on each muffin. Set aside. Top with poached egg and hollandaise sauce (recipes on page 83) and serve warm.

Serves 2.

Fried Green Tomato Benedict With Cajun Hollandaise

Ingredients

Fried Green Tomatoes

2 large, firm green tomatoes, sliced into 1/4 inch slices
1/2 teaspoon salt
1/4 teaspoon black pepper
3/4 cup flour
1 egg
1/2 cup milk
1 cup dried bread crumbs
1 cup panko bread crumbs
2-3 tablespoons bacon grease (or other oil for frying)

Poached Eggs

Recipe on page 83

Blender Cajun Hollandaise

1/2 cup butter
3 egg yolks
1 tablespoon lemon juice
1/2 teaspoon Cajun seasoning
1 tablespoon chopped parsley

Directions

Preheat oven to warm. Place a cooling rack on top of a baking sheet. Sprinkle both sides of tomatoes with salt and pepper.

Set up an assembly line. Place flour in a bowl and set aside. Whisk egg and milk together in a separate bowl. Combine plain dry bread crumbs and panko bread crumbs together in another bowl.

Dip each tomato in flour, then egg/milk mixture followed by bread crumbs until coated. Repeat until all tomatoes are coated.

Heat bacon grease in a skillet over medium heat. Drop a couple bread crumbs into the grease and if it sizzles, it is ready. Fry tomatoes in batches until golden on each side, about 3 minutes.

Transfer fried green tomatoes to cooling rack, sprinkle lightly with salt and place in warm oven until ready to use.

To make the hollandaise, melt butter over medium heat until it becomes foamy. Combine egg yolks, lemon juice and Cajun seasoning in a blender. Blend at medium-high speed until it lightens in color, about 30 seconds. Lower the blender speed to low and slowly drizzle in the melted butter and blend until the mixture becomes smooth and creamy, about 2 minutes.

Place blender in a bowl of lukewarm water to keep the hollandaise sauce warm while you poach the eggs.

To poach the eggs, heat water in a large skillet just until simmering. Add in a splash of vinegar. Working with just one egg, crack it into a small bowl. Hold the bowl just above the hot water and gently slide the egg in. Use a spoon to nudge the egg whites closer to the yolk so that they stay together. Keep the water at a simmer and repeat with remaining eggs. Turn off heat. Cover and let sit for 4 minutes or until the egg whites are cooked and the yolk is still soft. Use a slotted spoon to remove the eggs from the water.

To assemble the eggs benedict, place 2 fried green tomatoes on top of each other. Top with one egg. Spoon hollandaise over the top. Top with chopped parsley. Serve.

Serves 4.

Crab Cake Benedict

Ingredients

1 tablespoon unsalted butter
1/2 teaspoon minced garlic
1/4 cup finely chopped celery
1/4 cup finely chopped onion
pinch of red chili flakes (optional)
1/2 teaspoon flour
1/4 cup whipping cream
1 tablespoon chopped flat-leaf parsley
1 pound shelled, cooked Dungeness crab
3 tablespoons mayonnaise
1 large egg yolk
1 teaspoon Dijon mustard
1/4 teaspoon kosher salt
1/4 teaspoon black pepper
1/3 cup panko plus 1 1/2 to 2 cups for coating
6 to 8 large eggs (to match the number of crab cakes)
3 tablespoons canola oil (or vegetable)

Directions

Make crab cakes: Melt butter in a large frying pan over low heat. Add garlic, celery and onion and cook, stirring often, until translucent but not browned, 8 to 10 minutes. Add chili flakes and flour. Cook, stirring until flour smells toasted, about 30 seconds. Stir in cream and parsley. Remove from heat and let mixture cool.

Meanwhile, gently squeeze water from crab over a colander. In a medium bowl, whisk together mayonnaise, egg yolk, mustard, salt and black pepper. Stir in 1/3 cup panko, crab and cream mixture.

Put about 2 cups panko on a large plate. Form crab mixture into 1/2 or 1/3 cup patties (for 6 or 8 crab cakes). One at a time, set patties in panko, press lightly to help bread crumbs adhere and turn. Press lightly on second side. Transfer to a large plate, cover and chill at least 1 hour or up to 1 day.

Meanwhile, cook poached eggs as directed (recipe on page 83).

Heat oil in a large frying pan over medium heat. Cook crab cakes, turning only once, until dark golden brown on both sides, 8 to 10 minutes total. (If making 8 crab cakes, you may need to cook in batches; if so, wipe out pan and add a fresh 3 tablespoons oil for second batch.) Transfer to a plate and put in a 200 degree oven to keep warm.

Make hollandaise sauce as directed (recipe on page 83).

Put crab cakes on plates and slip a poached egg on each. Spoon about 1 1/2 tablespoons hollandaise sauce on top of each. Sprinkle with chives.

Serves 4.

Salmon Cake Benedict

Ingredients

2 (14.75 oz) cans salmon, drained

3/4 cup panko or breadcrumbs

1/2 cup minced fresh parsley

2 eggs, beaten

2 green onions, chopped

2 teaspoons creole seasoning

1 1/2 teaspoons ground black pepper

1 1/2 teaspoons garlic powder

3 tablespoons Worcestershire sauce

3 tablespoons grated Parmesan cheese

2 tablespoons Dijon mustard

2 tablespoons mayonnaise

1 tablespoon olive oil, or as needed, divided

Directions

In a large bowl, combine all ingredients, except for olive oil. Divide and shape into eight patties.

Heat enough olive oil in a large skillet to cover the cooking surface over medium heat. Fry salmon patties in batches until browned, 5 to 7 minutes per side. Repeat with more olive oil, as needed. Prepare poached eggs and hollandaise sauce as directed on page 83.

Quiche Lorraine

Ingredients

1 9 inch deep dish refrigerated or frozen pie crust, thawed
8 thick slices of bacon
1/2 cup half and half
1/4 cup heavy cream
2 eggs
1/2 teaspoon salt
1/2 cup shredded swiss cheese
1 tablespoon chopped chives

Directions

Preheat oven to 350 degrees.

Bake pie crust by placing a sheet of parchment paper on top of the crust and gently press it down until it covers the bottom and sides of crust. Fill with pie weights and bake 7-10 minutes or until shell is lightly browned. Remove from oven and allow to cool.

Meanwhile, cook bacon, drain on paper towels and dice up into small pieces. Set aside.

Whisk eggs and salt together vigorously, slowly adding in half and half and cream. Arrange bacon and cheese on the bottom of the pie crust. Gently pour the milk mixture over the top.

Bake on a cookie sheet for 40-45 minutes. The quiche should have a slight jiggle to it and will finish setting as it cools.

Serves 6.

Western Quiche

Ingredients

1 9 inch deep dish refrigerated or frozen pie crust, thawed
4 green onions, thinly sliced
1/3 cup chopped green bell pepper
1/3 cup chopped red bell pepper
1 jalapeno, diced
2 tablespoons butter
4 oz smoked ham chopped and divided
1 1/2 cups colby jack cheese, divided
1 cup heavy cream
6 large eggs
1 teaspoon garlic salt
1/2 teaspoon black pepper
1/2 teaspoon onion powder
1/4 teaspoon ground mustard

Directions

Preheat the oven to 375 degrees. Prick the bottom of pie shell using a fork. Bake for 5-7 minutes. Set aside.

In a small skillet melt the butter. Cook the sliced green onion, green pepper and red pepper until softened, 2-3 minutes. Add jalapeno. Set aside.

Layer half of the ham and half of the shredded cheese on the bottom of the pie shell. Whisk together heavy cream, eggs and seasonings until fully combined. Add cooked vegetables. Pour half over the first layer of ham and cheese then repeat ham, cheese and egg mixture. Place on a baking sheet bake for 10 minutes. Lower oven temperature to 350 degrees and continue to bake for an additional 30-40 minutes. Rest on a cooling rack for at least 30 minutes before serving.

Serves 6.

Farmer's Quiche

Ingredients

1 9 inch deep dish refrigerated or frozen pie crust, thawed
2 cups assorted tomatoes, cut into 1/2-inch thick slices and drained on a paper towel
1 tablespoon olive oil
2 small zucchini, sliced 1/2 inch thick
1/4 of a red onion, sliced thin
4 large eggs
1 cup half-and-half
1/4 cup flour
1/2 teaspoon salt
1/4 teaspoon dry mustard powder
1/2 teaspoon fresh ground pepper
1/4 teaspoon cayenne pepper
1 tablespoon fresh basil, chopped, plus extra for garnish
1 cup shredded Gruyere cheese
Paprika

Directions

Preheat oven to 350 degrees.

Bake crust for 10 minutes with pie weights or by pricking the bottom of the crust with a fork before baking. Set aside to cool.

Slice the tomatoes and place on a paper towel lined plate to drain. Heat olive oil in a large skillet over medium heat. Add zucchini in a single layer, season with salt and pepper and cook until lightly browned. Remove to a plate and add onion to the hot skillet. Cook 3-5 minutes or until lightly browned. Add the cooked onions to zucchini and set aside.

In a medium mixing bowl, whisk together eggs, half-and-half, flour, chopped basil, salt, pepper, cayenne and dry mustard.

Sprinkle shredded cheese in the bottom of the baked crust. Layer half the tomatoes and zucchini over the cheese. Gently pour the egg mixture over the vegetables. Top with the remaining tomatoes, zucchini and onions.

Sprinkle with paprika and bake for 30 minutes or until the egg mixture is set in the center. Tent the quiche with aluminum foil during baking if the crust browns too quickly.

Remove from the oven and allow the quiche to cool for 10-15 minutes before serving. It may also be served at room temperature. Store in the refrigerator.

Serves 6.

Ham and Cheese Quiche

Ingredients

1 9 inch deep dish refrigerated or frozen pie crust, thawed
1 tablespoon unsalted butter
1/2 medium yellow onion, diced
4 eggs, beaten
3/4 cup half and half
1/4 teaspoon salt
1/4 teaspoon black pepper
1 cup diced, cooked ham
1/2 cup shredded swiss cheese
1/2 cup shredded sharp cheddar cheese
2 tablespoon chives

Directions

Preheat oven to 400 degrees. Line a cookie sheet with foil or parchment. Bake pie crust for 10-15 minutes. Remove from oven and cool.

Melt butter in a small nonstick pan and cook onion on low heat with salt and pepper until caramelized (about 25-30 minutes). While onion is cooking whisk together in a large bowl the eggs, half and half and chives.

Scatter diced ham on the bottom of pie crust. Add caramelized onion evenly on top of the ham. Next, sprinkle cheese on top and pour egg mixture over the cheese. Reduce heat to 375 degrees and bake quiche 40-50 minutes or until set.
Note: If crust is browning too quickly, use foil to cover the edges of the crust and continue to bake until set.

Deluxe Breakfast Sandwiches

Ingredients

2 english muffins or biscuits, split
4 hashbrown patties
Oil for frying
4 slices cheddar cheese
2 eggs, over easy
1 tablespoon butter
2 sausage patties

Directions

Cook sausage patties on medium heat in a large frying pan. Drain on paper towels and set aside. Heat oil on medium heat in separate frying pan or cast iron pan until temperature is 325 degrees. Cook hashbrown patties 3-5 minutes on each side or until golden brown. Drain on paper towel.

Cook eggs with 1 tablespoon butter until desired doneness (usually over easy).

Toast english muffins or split biscuits and start stacking with one slice of cheese, hashbrown patty, egg, sausage patty and top with another slice of cheese then the muffin or biscuit top.

Note: I love to put salsa on these sandwiches or spread Aardvark Hot Sauce on the bottom of the biscuit or english muffin before adding all the toppings.

Makes 2 sandwiches.

Fried Chicken and Waffle Sandwich

Ingredients

Sandwiches

4 medium to large waffles
4 slices cheddar cheese
4 slices thick cut pepper bacon, cooked

Fried Chicken

2 cups buttermilk
3 teaspoons salt
Dash Aardvark Hot Sauce
2 chicken breasts, each sliced in half lengthwise (2 cutlets each)
1 1/2 cups flour
1 teaspoon salt
1/2 teaspoon garlic powder
1/2 teaspoon onion powder
1/4 teaspoon black pepper
1/4 teaspoon cayenne pepper
Oil for frying

Cajun Honey Butter

2 tablespoons pureed chipotle peppers in adobo sauce
1 teaspoon honey
8 ounces softened unsalted butter
salt and pepper to taste

Directions

Up to 12 hours prior to cooking the chicken, whisk buttermilk, salt, and hot sauce in a large bowl. Place chicken into the buttermilk brine. Cover and refrigerate.

Make the waffle batter (use your favorite homemade belgian waffle recipe or Krusteaz).

Place a baking sheet in the oven and preheat to 200 degrees. Preheat the waffle iron. Prepare the waffles according to manufacturer's directions, spraying the iron with cooking spray or brushing with oil prior to preparing each waffle. When the waffles are fully cooked, place in the preheated oven until ready to serve.

Fried Chicken: Pour about 2 inches of oil into a 10-inch skillet and preheat over medium-high. Whisk together the flour, salt, onion and garlic powder, cayenne pepper and black pepper together in a pie pan.

Using tongs, remove one piece of chicken at a time from the brine. Dip into flour on both sides, then dip back into the buttermilk and back into the flour. Fry on each side for about five minutes, until golden. Remove to a plate lined with paper towels. If not serving immediately, place on a baking sheet in the oven to keep warm.

Cajun Honey Butter: Combine all ingredients in a small saucepan on medium heat. Once melted, turn off the heat and set aside.

Cook eggs to your preference.

Assemble sandwiches

Place two waffles on a board or serving tray. Place one of the eggs on top of each waffle. Add chicken, two slices each of cheddar cheese, then top with remaining waffles to sandwich together.

Serve cajun honey butter on the side for dunking or to drizzle over the top of each sandwich.

Makes 2 sandwiches.

Loaded Fried Chicken Sandwich

Ingredients

2 large buttermilk biscuits

4 slices sharp cheddar cheese

4 slices thick cut pepper bacon

2 large pieces of Fried chicken (recipe on page 98)

1 cup sausage or bacon gravy (sausage gravy page 113, bacon gravy page 111)

Directions

Split buttermilk biscuits in half. Layer one slice of cheddar cheese, 2 strips of bacon, chicken and another slice cheese. Ladle half of the gravy on top and add other half of the biscuit. Serve with Aardvark Hot Sauce on the side.

Makes 2 sandwiches.

Breakfast Bagels
With Cream Cheese Variations

Ingredients

8 oz cream cheese, whipped

4 bagels, sliced and toasted

4 eggs, over easy

8 slices thick cut bacon (or 4 sausage patties)

4 slices cheddar cheese

Directions

Spread cream cheese over toasted bagels. Cook bacon or sausage in a medium sized frying pan, drain on paper towels and set aside.

Layer the meat on the bottom of the bagel. Add cheese and top with egg. Finish with top half of the bagel. See variations for fun flavors and combinations. Try a sweet and savory combination or just go completely savory with some of these spreads.

Spreads

Spicy Cream Cheese

8 oz softened cream cheese
1/2 tablespoon ancho chili powder
1/2 tablespoon granulated garlic
1 teaspoon red chili flakes
1/2 teaspoon cumin
4 roasted jalapeno peppers

Directions

Roast jalapeno peppers over the stove on high heat until it's blistered or broil in the oven until the outside skin is blistered and peppers are roasted. Cool about 15-20 minutes.

In a medium mixing bowl add remaining ingredients. Finely dice jalapeno and add to cream cheese mixture. Beat on medium speed until well combined.

Refrigerate at least 2-3 hours before serving or overnight.

Cranberry Nut Spread

8 oz cream cheese
2 tablespoons honey
3/4 cup dried cranberries, finely chopped
1/2 cup toasted walnuts, finely chopped
1 tablespoon finely grated orange zest
1/2 tablespoon fresh squeezed orange juice

Directions

Place all ingredients in a large mixing bowl and beat on medium speed until well combined. Refrigerate until ready to use.

Pumpkin Spread

8 oz cream cheese
2 tablespoons pumpkin puree
1 1/2 teaspoons pumpkin pie spice

Directions

Place all ingredients in a large mixing bowl and beat on medium speed until well combined. Refrigerate until ready to use.

Bleu Cheese & Bacon

8 oz cream cheese
2 oz soft bleu cheese
1 tablespoon honey
2 slices cooked bacon, finely chopped

Directions

Place all ingredients in a large mixing bowl and beat on medium speed until well combined. Refrigerate at least 2-3 hours or overnight.

Sweet Cinnamon

8 oz cream cheese
1/4 cup toasted walnuts, finely chopped
2 tablespoons light brown sugar, firmly packed
2 teaspoons cinnamon
1/2 teaspoon nutmeg
1/2 teaspoon vanilla

Directions

Place all ingredients in a large mixing bowl and beat on medium speed until well combined. Refrigerate until ready to use.

Mixed Berry

8 oz cream cheese
1/4 cup fresh strawberries, diced
1/4 cup blackberries, diced
1/4 cup raspberries, diced

Directions

Beat cream cheese in a medium mixing bowl on high speed until soft and fluffy. Gently fold in the berries. Refrigerate until ready to use.

Savory Bacon

8 oz cream cheese
6 thick slices pepper bacon, cooked and finely chopped
1/4 cup chives
1/4 cup sun dried tomatoes
Salt and pepper to taste

Directions
Add all ingredients to a large mixing bowl and beat on medium speed with a hand mixer until well combined. Refrigerate at least 2-3 hours or overnight before using for best flavor.

Loaded Breakfast Bagels

Ingredients

Sandwiches

4 slices bacon
4 slices pickled jalapeno
2 bagels, sliced in half
2 eggs
2 slices cheddar cheese
1/2 avocado, cut into slices
1 large beefsteak tomato, sliced

Spicy Cream Cheese

2 8-oz packages of cream cheese, softened
2 green onions, sliced
1/3 cup red onion, diced
1/4 red bell pepper, diced
1/4 green bell pepper, diced
1/2 clove garlic, minced
1/4 cup green chiles, diced
dash of salt

Directions

Spicy Cream Cheese: Place all ingredients, except cream cheese and salt, into a food processor and pulse until vegetables are finely minced.

Add cream cheese and salt, pulse to reach desired consistency. Transfer to a covered container and refrigerate several hours to allow flavors to blend.

Bagels: Cook bacon on medium heat in a large skillet until crisp, about 7-10 minutes. Remove and drain on a plate lined with paper towels and cover to keep warm. Toast bagels in oven or toaster.

Cook eggs over easy or over medium in the same skillet. Prepare spicy cream cheese (can be made the day before as well), spread evenly over the bottom and top of the bagel slices. Add half of the cooked bacon, one slice of tomato, 1 cooked egg, slice of cheese, avocado and jalapenos.

Makes 2 sandwiches.

World's Best Breakfast Burritos

Ingredients

8 oz pork breakfast sausage
8 oz thick cut pepper bacon
1 package frozen hash brown breakfast potatoes (cubes or tater tots)
1 red bell pepper, diced
1 green bell pepper, diced
2 jalapenos, sliced thin
4 tablespoons unsalted butter
8 large eggs, whisked
1/4 teaspoon kosher salt
1/4 teaspoon coarse, black pepper
10 large flour tortillas
1 cup sharp cheddar cheese, shredded
1 cup pepperjack cheese, shredded
2 large avocados, diced
1/2 cup pico de gallo
Sour cream, to serve

Directions

Preheat oven to 300 degrees.

Spray a large cookie sheet with nonstick spray and set aside.

Add pork sausage to a large cast iron skillet on medium heat and cook through, crumbling it up until no longer pink. Transfer cooked sausage to prepared baking sheet and place in oven to keep warm.

Note: the same skillet can be used for cooking each of these ingredients. Wipe out the pan to remove any excess grease before cooking each ingredient.

Cook bacon and drain on paper towels. Chop into bite size pieces and place in the oven with cooked pork on the same pan.

Fry the potatoes on medium heat in the skillet with 2 tablespoons of oil until golden and crispy. Drain on paper towels and place in oven with sausage and bacon.

Add 2 tablespoons of oil in the skillet and cook bell peppers until soft. Add salt, pepper and jalapeno slices. Cook additional 2-3 minutes or until soft. Place in oven with meat and potatoes.

Add 4 tablespoons butter in the skillet and cook eggs until scrambled, about **2-3 minutes**. Remove and season with salt and pepper.

Remove baking sheet from the oven.

To assemble the burritos, layer the tortilla with the cheeses, eggs, vegetable mixture, meat and hashbrowns. Add diced avocado, pico de gallo and sour cream.

Makes 10 large burritos.

Note: *This may look like a lot of work but this recipe will make A LOT of burritos! You can wrap each burrito individually with plastic wrap and freeze them for future breakfasts! Just omit the avocado, sour cream, and salsa.*

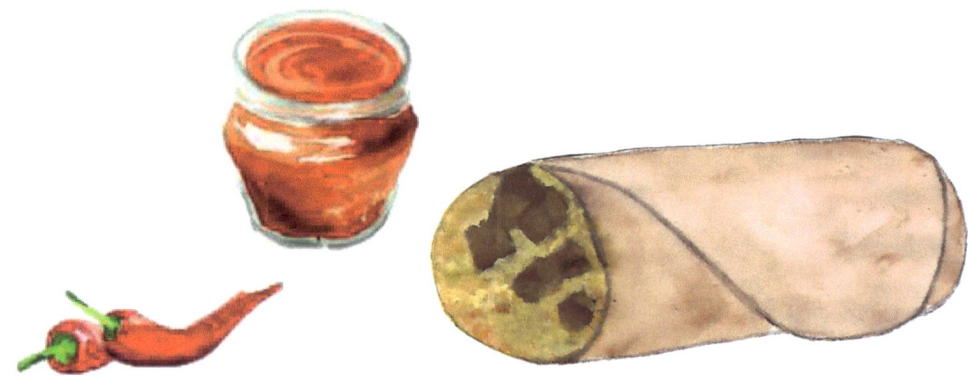

Turkey Bacon Spinach Wraps

Ingredients

8 oz fresh spinach
1 oz sundried tomatoes, finely chopped
4 oz low fat cream cheese
6 slices turkey bacon
10 egg whites
1 teaspoon oregano
1/2 teaspoon garlic powder
1/4 teaspoon salt
4 whole wheat (or spinach) burrito size tortillas
4 oz feta cheese, crumbled

Directions

Heat a medium sized saucepan over medium heat and cook spinach until wilted, about 6-10 minutes. Remove from heat and allow to cool slightly, about 20 minutes.

Place wilted spinach in a bowl and mix in cream cheese, sundried tomatoes, oregano, garlic powder and salt.

Add egg whites to a small pan, lightly greased with nonstick spray on low heat and cook until soft.

Cook bacon on medium low heat in a separate frying pan until crisp, about 7-10 minutes. Drain on paper towels. Cut into bite size pieces.

Spread spinach mixture on a tortilla then top with egg whites, bacon, and feta cheese. Roll the tortilla up tight (like a burrito), cut in half and serve.

Makes 4 wraps.

SECTION 6
Side Dishes

Fluffy Biscuits and Bacon Gravy

Ingredients

Biscuits

1 1/2 cups + 3 tablespoons flour
1 teaspoon sugar
1/4 teaspoon salt
2 teaspoons baking powder
1/2 teaspoon cream of tartar
6 tablespoons cold butter
1 egg, lightly beaten
1/2 cup milk

Gravy

2 tablespoons bacon grease
1 tablespoon flour
1 1/2 cups heavy cream or half and half
4 slices thick cut bacon
salt and pepper, to taste
1/2 teaspoon cayenne pepper
1 tablespoon parsley (for garnish)

Directions

Biscuits

Preheat oven to 450 degrees. Line cookie sheet with parchment paper and spray lightly with nonstick cooking spray.

Combine the dry ingredients in a medium sized bowl. Using a pastry cutter, cut in butter until coarse and crumbly. Add milk and egg. Mix until well combined, do not overmix. Dough should be sticky.

Turn the dough out onto a generously floured surface. Sprinkle flour on top of the dough so it won't stick to your fingers and knead 10-15 times. Sprinkle more flour on the dough if needed. Roll or pat dough into 3/4-1 inch thickness.

Using a biscuit cutter, cut out 6-8 biscuits and place on baking sheet about 1 inch apart. Bake 8-10 minutes or until golden brown.

Gravy:

Cook bacon until crisp, dice into small pieces and set aside. Add flour to bacon drippings and cook on low heat 4-5 minutes until lightly browned. Slowly whisk in cream, whisking continuously.

Let mixture come to a low boil, add seasoning (for more flavor, add plenty of pepper, to taste).

Stir in bacon and simmer additional 5-8 minutes on low heat.

To Serve:

Cut biscuit in half, pour gravy over each biscuit and top with fresh parsley.

Serves 6-8.

Sausage Gravy

Ingredients

1 teaspoon vegetable oil
1 large onion, minced
1 pound bulk breakfast sausage
2 tablespoons unsalted butter
1/2 cup flour
2 cups whipping cream, room temperature
1/3 cup water
2 cups whole milk, room temperature
1 1/2 teaspoons sea salt
1/2 teaspoon freshly ground black pepper
2 teaspoons finely chopped fresh sage

Directions

Heat vegetable oil in a large 3 to 4 quart saucepan over medium heat. Add onion and cook until translucent. Add sausage and cook until browned, breaking into chunks as it cooks. Reduce heat to low. Drain excess grease, return to pan and set aside.

Melt butter in a small saucepan over medium-low heat. Slowly add flour, stirring, until a smooth paste forms. This is your roux. Continue cooking, stirring often, until light brown, about 10 minutes. (If the roux becomes too thick or clumpy, stir in a splash of cream.)

Add 1/3 cup water to the sausage. Increase heat to medium-high. When the mixture reaches a simmer, stir in roux a little at a time. Reduce heat to medium and slowly add cream and milk. Bring to a simmer and cook, stirring frequently, until gravy reaches desired thickness. Add salt, black pepper and sage. Serve immediately.

Makes about 6 cups.

Stuffed Hashbrowns

Ingredients

4 cups frozen shredded hashbrowns

1/2 cup sour cream

1/2 cup shredded cheddar cheese

1/4 cup diced, cooked bacon

1/4 white onion, diced

1 tablespoon chives

4 tablespoons butter

1 teaspoon cajun spice

salt and pepper to taste

4 tablespoons Oil for frying

Directions

Heat oven to 400 degrees. Heat oil in a medium sized skillet on medium high heat. Cook hashbrowns 5-8 minutes on one side, flip and cook another 5-8 minutes.

In a separate pan on medium heat, melt butter. Add onion and cook until tender about 8-10 minutes. Set aside. In a small bowl, add sour cream and chives. Stir well to combine.

Place hashbrowns flat on lightly greased cookie sheet and sprinkle cheese, cooked bacon and onion on top. Bake 10 minutes or until cheese has melted. Scoop sour cream mixture onto one side of the hashbrowns and fold over. Serve immediately.

Serves 4.

Chicken Fried Bacon

Ingredients

12 slices thick-cut bacon

2 eggs

1/3 cup milk

1 cup flour

freshly cracked black pepper

Vegetable oil

Directions

In a small bowl, whisk together eggs and milk. Place flour in a separate shallow bowl and season generously with black pepper. Dredge bacon in flour first, then egg mixture, then back in flour.

In a large skillet over medium heat, heat oil (it should reach 1" up the side of pan) until a pinch of flour starts to bubble when added to oil. Add bacon and fry until golden, about 2 minutes per side. Transfer to a paper towel-lined plate to cool slightly.

Serve bacon with gravy on the side for dipping or drizzle caramel sauce over the top.

Serves 4.

Sweet and Spicy Bacon

Ingredients

1 lb thick cut bacon
6 tablespoons brown sugar
1 1/2 teaspoons cayenne pepper
1 teaspoon cracked black pepper
1 1/2 teaspoons red pepper flakes

Directions

Preheat oven to 350 degrees and line a large baking sheet with parchment paper or foil.

In a small mixing bowl add brown sugar, cayenne pepper, pepper flakes, and cracked black pepper. Mix well.

Lay each strip of bacon on the lined baking sheet. Press brown sugar mixture into the bacon. The coating will bake into the bacon so you won't need to add more coating on the other side.

Bake for 25-35 minutes or until crispy.

Serves 6.

Pudding Fruit Salad

Ingredients

1 container (4 oz) refrigerated vanilla pudding
1/2 cup whipped topping
1/4 cup maraschino cherries, drained
1 1/2 cups miniature marshmallows
1 can (11 oz) mandarin oranges, drained
1 can (8 oz) pineapple tidbits, drained
1 cup fresh strawberries, sliced

Directions

In a medium bowl, mix pudding and whipped cream. Gently fold in remaining ingredients. Serve immediately or store in refrigerator up to 8 hours.

Serves 6-8

Glazed Fruit Salad

Ingredients

1 can pineapple chunks, in juice
1 can mandarin oranges, drained
2 bananas, sliced
2 cups mixed berries of your choice
1 small box vanilla instant pudding

Directions

In a large mixing bowl add pineapple chunks with juice and box of vanilla pudding. Stir well to combine. Add remaining ingredients. Store in refrigerator until ready to serve.

Serves 6-8

Strawberry Cheesecake Fruit Salad

Ingredients

1 box instant cheesecake pudding mix
12 oz Cool Whip
18 oz strawberry yogurt
1 lb fresh strawberries, sliced
3 cups miniature marshmallows

Directions

In a large bowl add pudding mix, Cool Whip and yogurt. Stir well to combine. Refrigerate overnight or at least 4 hours. Fold in remaining ingredients.

Serve immediately.

Serves 6-8.

Skillet Fried Apples

Ingredients

4 apples, peeled, cored and sliced
2 tablespoons bacon drippings
2 tablespoons butter or margarine
2 tablespoons brown sugar
1 teaspoon cinnamon
1/2 teaspoon nutmeg
1 teaspoon salt

Directions

In a skillet over medium heat, add bacon drippings and margarine. Add apple slices, brown sugar, cinnamon, nutmeg and salt. Stir well so apples are covered with spices and brown sugar. Bring to a boil and cover. Reduce heat to simmer and cook 20-25 minutes until apples are soft, but not mushy.

Serves 4

Brulee'd Oatmeal With Fresh Berries

Ingredients

3 cups water

1/4 teaspoon kosher salt

1 1/2 cups quick cooking oats

1 vanilla bean pod

4 tablespoons brown sugar

6 oz assorted berries of choice

Directions

In a small saucepan bring water and salt to a boil. Add oats and stir well to combine. Split vanilla bean and scrape the seeds into the water with the oats. Add the whole pod for more flavor. Reduce heat and cook for 3-5 minutes.

Cover and remove from heat and let set until desired consistency. Remove vanilla pod.

Divide oatmeal among four broiler-proof bowls. Sprinkle 1 tablespoon of sugar over each dish and place under broiler. Broil until sugar caramelizes and forms a crust, about 3 to 4 minutes.

Watch carefully so sugar doesn't burn. Serve immediately with cream and berries or topping of your choice.

Serves 4.

French Style Hot Chocolate

Thick, luxurious, rich hot chocolate. Best served with a warm croissant for dipping.

Ingredients

1 1/2 cups whole milk
1/2 cup heavy cream
2 teaspoons powdered sugar
1/2 teaspoon espresso powder (dissolved in 1 teaspoon hot water) optional, but delicious for intensifying chocolate flavor
8 oz bittersweet (high quality) chocolate, at least 70%, chopped
Whipped cream

Directions

In a medium saucepan over medium heat, whisk together whole milk, heavy cream, powdered sugar and espresso until small bubbles appear around the edges. Do not allow the mixture to boil.

Remove saucepan from heat and stir in chopped **chocolate** until melted. Return sauce to low heat, if needed, for the chocolate to melt completely. Serve warm with whipped cream.

Makes 2 cups.

Frozen Caramel Macchiato

Ingredients

3/4 cup freshly brewed espresso
2/3 cup milk
1 pump Torani Caramel Syrup
3 tablespoons caramel sauce
2 cups ice

Directions

Add first 4 ingredients into a large blender and blend until well combined. Add ice and blend until smooth.

Pour into a large glass and serve with whipped cream and a drizzle of caramel sauce on top.

Serves 1.

Frozen "Hot Chocolate"

Ingredients

3 oz high quality milk chocolate
2 teaspoons hot chocolate mix
1 1/2 tablespoons sugar
1 1/2 cups milk
3 cups ice
Whipped cream
Chocolate dessert sauce or syrup

Directions

Melt milk chocolate over medium heat in a small saucepan. Add hot chocolate mix and sugar.

Remove from heat and slowly whisk in the milk. Let cool to room temperature.

Add ice, remaining milk and chocolate mixture to a blender. Blend until smooth. Pour into a large glass, top with whipped cream and a drizzle of rich chocolate sauce or syrup on top.

Serves 1.

Slow Cooker Apple Cider

Ingredients

8-10 medium sized apples, assorted
1 orange
3 cinnamon sticks
2 teaspoons whole cloves
8-10 cups water (depending on size of slow cooker)
2/3 cup light brown sugar

Directions

Wash apples and the orange, cut into quarters. No need to remove stems or seeds. Add fruit and spices to a large slow cooker. Add water until it's about an inch from the top of the bowl. Cook on high for 4 hours or low for 8 hours.

During the last hour of the cooking process, remove lid and mash fruit with a potato masher. Turn off heat. Strain cider to remove all of the fruit and seeds. Pour cider back into the slow cooker and add brown sugar, stirring well to combine. Cook on low until ready to serve.

OPTIONAL: Add 1/4 cup caramel syrup to the slow cooker after straining the fruit. Top with whipped cream.

Makes approximately one half gallon.

Smoothies

Simple smoothies! Add all ingredients to a large blender and blend until smooth.

Banana Berry

3/4 cup apple juice
1/4 cup strawberry nectar
2/3 cup frozen strawberries
1 banana, sliced
1 scoop raspberry sherbet
1 scoop vanilla frozen yogurt
1/2 cup ice

Strawberry Orange

1 can frozen orange juice
2/3 cup frozen strawberries
1 banana, sliced
2 scoops vanilla frozen yogurt
1/2 cup ice

Citrus Delight

1 cup fresh orange juice
1/2 cup pineapple juice
1 scoop orange sherbet
1 scoop vanilla frozen yogurt
1/2 cup frozen strawberries

Peachy Keen

12 oz peach nectar
1 1/2 cups frozen peaches
1 banana, sliced
2 scoops orange sherbet
1/2 cup ice

Classic Mimosa

Ingredients

1 (750 ml) bottle chilled champagne
3 cups freshly squeezed orange juice
1/2 cup Grand Marnier, optional

Directions

Fill 8 champagne flutes half full with chilled champagne. Top with orange juice. Add 1 tablespoon of Grand Marnier to each glass, if desired.

Makes 8 drinks.

Peach Bellini

Ingredients

Peach Puree

2 medium sized peaches, peeled and diced
1/2 cup water

Bellini

1 tablespoon lemon juice
1/2 teaspoon honey
12 oz chilled prosecco or champagne

Directions

Peach Purée: Blend peaches with water. Leave in blender to create the rest of the bellini mixture.

Peach Bellini: Add lemon juice and honey to peach purée and blend until smooth. Fill a stemless glass or champagne flute a quarter full, top with chilled champagne or prosecco. Garnish with a peach slice.

Makes 6 Drinks.

Raspberry Limoncello

Ingredients

1 bottle chilled Prosecco or champagne
1 cup Limoncello
1 cup raspberries, *muddled and for garnish*
2 lemons, *for garnish*

Directions

Coat the rim of 6 stemless wine glasses with sugar. At the bottom of each wine glass, muddle 4-5 raspberries.

Fill each glass halfway with Prosecco or champagne, then fill with Limoncello. Garnish with fresh sliced lemon and raspberries before serving.

Makes 6 drinks.

Brunch Punch

Ingredients

2 cups orange juice
1 cup cranberry juice
2 liters Ginger Ale
1/4 cup orange liqueur
1 cup strawberries, sliced
1 cup blueberries
1 (750ml) bottle champagne

Directions

Combine all of the ingredients, except the champagne, in a large punch bowl or serving bowl and stir well to combine. Slowly add champagne and stir to combine.

Serve immediately.

16-18 Servings.

INDEX

A
Apple Bran Muffins, **43**
Apple Cider Syrup, **12**
Apple Cinnamon Danish, **57**
Apple Cinnamon Pancakes, **6**
Apple Fritter Loaf, **61**
Apple Sour Cream Coffee Cake, **49**

B
Bacon Gravy, **111**
Banana Berry Smoothie, **128**
Banana Bran Muffins, **42**
Bananas Foster French Toast, **33**
Banana Walnut Bread, **59**
Basic Cream Scones, **44**
Basic Crepes, **14**
Better Than "Drakes" Mini Coffee Cakes, **55**
Birthday Cake Waffles, **22**
Bleu Cheese And Bacon Spread, **103**
Blintzes, **15**
Blueberry Buttermilk Pancakes, **8**
Blueberry Deluxe Muffins, **37**
Bran Muffins, **40**
Breakfast Bagels, **101**
Breakfast Pizza, **72**
Brulee'd Oatmeal With Fresh Berries, **120**
Brunch Punch, **130**
Bubble Waffles, **25**

C
Captain Crunch French Toast, **29**
Caramel Pecan Sticky Buns, **69**
Chicken Fried Bacon, **115**

Churro Waffles With Tres Leches Sauce, **23**
Cinnamon Roll Waffles, **20**
Citrus Delight Smoothie, **126**
Classic Eggs Benedict, **83**
Classic Mimosa, **127**
Country Skillet, **81**
Crab Cake Benedict, **87**
Cranberry Nut Spread, **102**
Creamy Egg and Bacon Au Gratin, **74**
Cronuts, **66**

D
Deluxe Breakfast Sandwiches, **97**
Double Chocolate Pancakes, **9**
Dutch Apple Pancakes, **11**

E
Easy Chocolate Croissants, **64**

F
Farmer's Quiche, **93**
Florentine Benedict, **84**
Fluffy Biscuits and Bacon Gravy, **111**
French Style Hot Chocolate, **122**
Fried Chicken and Waffle Sandwich, **98**
Fried Green Tomato Benedict, **85**
Frozen Caramel Macchiato, **123**
Frozen Hot Chocolate, **124**
Fruit and Cream Cheese Danish, **58**

G
Garden Fresh Frittata, **76**
German Pancakes, **13**
Glazed Fruit Salad, **118**

H
Ham and Cheese Breakfast Muffins, **39**
Ham and Cheese Quiche, **95**
Ham, Chile and Cheese Baked Omelet, **79**
Hawaiian French Toast, **30**

I

J
Jalapeno Bacon Cheese Scones, **48**

K

L
Leige Waffles, **18**
Lemon Coffee Cake, **51**
Lemon Loaf, **60**
Loaded Breakfast Bagels, **105**
Loaded Fried Chicken Sandwich, **100**

M
Marionberry Coffee Cake, **53**
Mediterranean Omelet, **78**
Mixed Berry Cream Cheese Spread, **104**
Mom's Best Donuts, **67**

N

O
Oreo Cheesecake Waffles, **21**
Overnight Creme Brulee French Toast, **28**
Overnight Marionberry French Toast, **34**

P
Pancake Puffs, **16**
Peach Bellini, **128**
Peachy Keen Smoothie, **126**
Pudding Filled Donut Holes, **65**
Pudding Fruit Salad, **117**
Puff Pancake, **10**
Pumpkin Bran Muffins, **41**
Pumpkin Bread, **62**
Pumpkin Cream Cheese Spread, **103**

Q
Quiche Lorraine, **90**

R
Raspberry Limoncello, **129**
Rich Buttermilk Waffles, **17**

S
Salmon Cake Benedict, **89**
Sausage Gravy, **113**
Savory Bacon Cream Cheese Spread, **104**
Simple Cinnamon Rolls, **68**
Skillet Fried Apples, **119**
Slow Cooker Apple Cider, **125**
Spicy Cream Cheese Spread, **102**
Strawberry Cheesecake French Toast, **31**
Strawberry Cheesecake Fruit Salad, **118**
Strawberry Orange Smoothie, **126**
Stuffed Hashbrowns, **114**
Stuffed Pancakes, **5**
Sweet and Spicy Bacon, **116**
Sweet Cinnamon Cream Cheese Spread, **103**

T
Traditional French Omelet, **80**
Triple Chocolate Scones, **46**
Triple Crunch French Toast, **27**
Turkey Bacon Spinach Wraps, **109**

U

V

W
Western Quiche, **92**
World's Best Breakfast Burritos, **107**

X

Y
Yorkshire "Pirate Eyes", **71**

Z

Copyright © 2019 by Sarah Gilbert

All rights reserved. This book or any portion thereof may not be reproduced or used in any manner whatsoever without the express written permission of the publisher except for the use of brief quotations in a book review or scholarly journal.

First Printing: 2019

www.ingramcontent.com/pod-product-compliance
Lightning Source LLC
Chambersburg PA
CBHW041156290426
44108CB00003B/90